TWICE

TWICE

THE STORY OF K-POP'S GREATEST GIRL GROUP

JAMIE HEAL

HarperCollins*Publishers*

HarperCollins*Publishers*
1 London Bridge Street
London SE1 9GF

HarperCollins*Publishers*
Macken House, 39/40 Mayor Street Upper
Dublin 1, D01 C9W8, Ireland

www.harpercollins.co.uk

First published by HarperCollins*Publishers* 2020

3 5 7 9 10 8 6 4 2

A catalogue record of this book is
available from the British Library

HB ISBN 978-0-00-840477-2
EB ISBN 978-0-00-840478-9

Printed and bound in the UK
using 100% renewable electricity at CPI Group (UK) Ltd

MIX
Paper | Supporting
responsible forestry
FSC™ C007454

This book is produced from independently certified FSC™ paper
to ensure responsible forest management.

For more information visit: www.harpercollins.co.uk/green

CONTENTS

An Intro to K-pop   1

PART ONE: THE TWICE STORY

1   6Mix and *Sixteen*   11
2   Debut   25
3   The Story Begins   35
4   Once   45
5   Cheer Up   55
6   A Winning Formula   65
7   One in a Million   75
8   Welcome to Twiceland   85
9   The Nation's Favourites   95
10 What is Love?   107
11 Summer Nights   119
12 Cheers and Tears   131
13 Feel Special   143
14 More & More   153

PART TWO: THE TWICE MEMBERS

15	Nayeon	165
16	Jeongyeon	173
17	Momo	181
18	Sana	189
19	Jihyo	197
20	Mina	205
21	Dahyun	213
22	Chaeyoung	221
23	Tzuyu	229

| | Picture Credits | 237 |
| | Index | 239 |

AN INTRO TO K-POP

Korean pop music – K-pop – is a broad term that covers a huge number of solo artists and groups. They are diverse in terms of musical genre – encompassing R'n'B, dance, hip-hop, ballads, rock and indie – and vary in style, size of group and, increasingly, nationality, with many groups having members from Japan, China and other countries. What nearly all these groups – including Twice – share is the culture of K-pop. This culture has grown over the last 20 years or so to produce and promote not only the music of these artists, but also their dance skills, their looks and their personalities. The following is a brief guide to some of the landmarks, concepts and events that may help anyone who is new to this fascinating genre to understand K-pop.

ENTERTAINMENT COMPANIES

Like Western record labels, entertainment companies are agencies that manage and fund the recordings and promotion of K-pop acts. There are many such companies, but for over ten years the so-called 'Big Three' – SM Entertainment, YG Entertainment and JYP Entertainment – have dominated K-pop, although recently BTS's company Big Hit Entertainment has become a major player. These companies manage groups, solo artists and actors, often under strict contracts which restrict activities such as diets, dating and social interactions.

TRAINEES

The entertainment companies are constantly scouting and auditioning for new talent. Often signed as young teenagers, those who are selected can spend many years intensively learning vocal, dance and other useful skills, such as languages, as well as attending school for their education. Being a trainee can be gruelling work, with monthly evaluations that can lead to many failing to make the grade and being rejected. Those who remain do so in the hope that they will be chosen by the company to 'debut' (see below).

GROUP ROLES AND LINES

K-pop groups commonly have four or more members. Although all will sing and dance, each will be given a specific role within the group. There will be singers, dancers and visuals (those whose looks alone get them noticed). Each group will have a leader (often, though not always, the oldest member) and a *maknae*, the youngest member, who is treated as the baby of the group and expected to be super-cute. Often, fans will also pick out sub-groups or 'lines', which can be based on their roles, such as the vocal line, being the same age and so sharing a birth year – as in the 98 line – their nationality – as seen in Twice's Japanese, or J-line – or any characteristics that link them.

DEBUT

The company – its producers, choreographers, stylists, vocal tutors and other experts – work with the selected members towards a launch date known as the debut. This debut is often make or break; a big chance to make an impression in a crowded market. Many companies will spend months preparing the ground for a debut. They will release teaser photos and videos of each member of the group in advance, or even clips or whole pre-debut videos. On debut day the act will perform at a special showcase, with media appearances and performances on music shows following over the next month.

IDOL

An idol is a mainstream K-pop star, as opposed to a hip-hop artist, rock musician or acts from other 'outsider' genres. Idols are expected to be multi-talented, able to act, sing, dance and look good. They are also expected to interact with fans, in person and on social media, and participate in variety shows.

AEGYO

Aegyo, pronounced 'egg-yo', is the use of cute voices, facial expressions and gestures to show affection or to flirt. Female (and some male) idols are expected to perform *aegyo* on variety shows, at fan meetings and in concerts. It can often take the form of baby voices, using hands to make symbols such as hearts or kisses, or creating a super-cute face by making pretend dimples or forming a 'V'-shaped chin.

GIRL CRUSH

Girl groups traditionally had a cute and innocent image, and often dressed in schoolgirl-style uniforms or girly, candy-coloured outfits. However, the 2010s groups, such as Miss A, f(x) and 2NE1, took on a more hard-edged, confident, individual and sexy image, more akin to that of Western artists. This vibe became known as 'girl crush'. As the decade progressed, some groups, such as Red Velvet and Girls' Generation, portrayed both cutesy and girl-crush concepts.

MUSIC SHOWS

There are music shows on national and cable South Korean television nearly every day. They have different formats, but all enable the groups to perform their latest release and sometimes other songs, too. They show music videos, but performances (even if groups often lip sync) in front of a live audience are an essential element. Each show also presents a prize to the most popular act – to 'win a music show' is the first ambition of any K-pop idol. Many shows often have Christmas or other seasonal specials in which groups can perform covers of hits or join other artists in one-off performances.

VARIETY SHOWS

Idols can show off their personalities and sense of fun by appearing on one of South Korea's numerous variety shows. These can be straightforward chat shows, but more often they involve challenges, games, pranks and opportunities for idols to demonstrate their skills. Shows such as *Weekly Idol*, *Running Man* and *Knowing Bros* feature popular dance games in which idols dance to other groups' choreography or speeded-up versions or randomly selected parts of their own songs.

V LIVE

Launched in 2015, this app provides a streaming service for K-pop fans. Artists are able to post videos or recordings and talk live to fans, who can themselves post comments which are sometimes read aloud in the stream. These livestreams can be advertised in advance or they may be impromptu broadcasts flagged by phone notifications. Twice are frequent users of the service. They often stream from their dorm, but also from concert dressing rooms, backstage at TV shows, from airports and even during taxi journeys. Many of the broadcasts are subtitled for international fans.

AWARD SHOWS

K-pop has a multitude of annual award shows that recognise artists' status, recordings and performances over the year. The most prestigious are MAMA (Mnet Asian Music Awards), MMA (Melon Music Awards), Korean Music Awards, Seoul Music Awards and the Golden Disc Awards. These are glittering events where idols pose for photographers on the red carpet and sit together in a VIP section. Many acts perform one or a medley of songs and fans loudly support their favourites. Awards are decided upon in various ways – usually sales, streams and online votes are included – so they often provoke controversy.

FANDOMS

K-pop fans support their artists with a passion, and established acts have their own fandoms with their own names. Twice have Once, BTS have Army and Blackpink have Blink. Anyone can belong to a fandom, there is no membership and members can participate as much or as little as they choose. Online forums are the main channel of communication where fans are urged to stream their group's videos, vote for them in music shows and awards, arrange chants and banners for concerts, and generally support the group's members. Fandoms often collect sizeable charity donations in the name of their idols.

COMEBACKS

An act doesn't need to have been absent for long to have a comeback, it's just the release and promotion of new material. Often this will be tied into a change of 'concept' – this can be anything from a new hair colour to a totally new musical genre, but often involves a theme that encompasses outfits, style and music.

GENERATIONS

K-pop is considered to have four generations. The first genera-tion emerged with the start of K-pop as we know it in the 1990s, with the pioneering Seo Taiji and Boys. It included girl-group successes S.E.S. and Fin.K.L. The second generation inspired the Korean Wave (*hallyu*) of the 2000s and gave birth to legends such as Girls' Generation, 2NE1 and Wonder Girls, while Big Bang and Super Junior were the most popular boy bands. The third generation was spearheaded by EXO and then BTS, and saw Twice as well as Blackpink, Red Velvet and others find international success, while from 2018 onwards, a fourth generation emerged, led by girl groups (G)I-dle, Iz★One and Itzy and boy bands Stray Kids and Ateez.

PART ONE

THE TWICE STORY

1

6MIX AND SIXTEEN

SEOUL, SOUTH KOREA: 18 OCTOBER 2015

Nine girls sit in front of the camera. They have been living together in an apartment – sharing two, three or four to a bedroom – for three months now. Their ages range from 16 to 19, their nationalities from Korean to Japanese to Taiwanese; some have been friends for years, others have only really known each other for six months. They look like any other group of teenage girls – very pretty teenage girls.

As the livestream begins, most of the talking is done by those in the front row, except the blonde girl in the centre who stares intently at the camera with her big round eyes. The four in the back row make supportive yelps and thumbs up and hearts and kisses with their fingers. They are all giggly, shy and very, very excited.

These girls are a new girl group and in two days' time they will be releasing their first ever single and EP. It will be the start of an incredible journey …

At the heart of the Twice story is a man in his forties named Park Jin-young. Often known by his initials, JYP, he is a South Korean singer-songwriter with three top ten albums and five top ten singles, including 'Who's Your Mama?', a 2015 number one hit. Born in 1971, he is a prolific songwriter and producer for many Korean artists and groups, but, most importantly in the Twice story, he is the founder and CEO of JYP Entertainment.

Park Jin-young founded JYP Entertainment in 1997, but it was the massive success of boy band g.o.d and singer Rain, both integral to the first *hallyu* wave of the early 2000s, that established the company as a major K-pop player. In 2007, JYP Entertainment launched its first girl group, Wonder Girls. Originally a five-member group with an average age of 16, they were a sensation. They mixed hip-hop, R'n'B and retro styles, constantly swapped visual concepts and had hit after hit, including their debut 'Irony', 'Tell Me' – which was propelled by member Sohee's iconic 'Omona' line – followed by 2008's 'So Hot' and 'Nobody'. They even became the first ever K-pop group to break into the US *Billboard* Hot 100 when 'Nobody' reached number 76. Wonder Girls dominated K-pop in the following years, with only SM Entertainment's Girls' Generation matching their success.

JYP Entertainment followed Wonder Girls with other success-ful launches, particularly another girl group, Miss A, and boy band 2PM. Miss A's debut 'Bad Girl, Good Girl' became a K-pop classic with singer Suzy destined to become the darling of the nation. JYP himself was a popular figure, making cameo appear-ances in music videos and on his artists' tracks, and he was always a welcome guest on TV variety shows. Among all the entertain-ment companies, JYP Entertainment enjoyed the best press. They had a reputation for treating trainees and their stars with respect. JYP was known for selecting idols for debut on the basis of their personality, not just their appearance, and listening to his idols' views and opinions. After all, JYP was still a recording artist himself.

K-pop never stands still, though, and by the end of 2013 things were not looking quite so rosy for JYP Entertainment. 2PM were still enjoying reasonable success, but on the girl-group side, both Wonder Girls and Miss A were in an extended hiatus and it wasn't known when or whether they would return. According to some, JYP Entertainment were in danger of losing their Big Three company status. They needed a major new act, so they debuted a new boy band, Got7, in January 2014, and announced plans for two new groups to debut in April: a boy band named 5Live (who would eventually debut in 2015 as Day6) and a girl group called 6Mix.

JYP Entertainment had high hopes for 6Mix. According to press information supplemented by rumour, the group was made up of six long-standing trainees. The first to be confirmed was American-Korean Lena, who at 20 was two years older than the others and had already featured as a rapper on Sunmi's 'Full Moon'. Then there was Cecilia, an Australian-Chinese trainee, and four long-standing Korean trainees: Jisoo (whose stage name was Jihyo), Jeongyeon, Nayeon and Minyoung. The group was well balanced, they had trained together for many years and were well prepared for their debut.

Then, on 16 April 2014, tragedy hit South Korea. A ferry bound for the holiday destination of Jeju Island, off the coast of Korea, sank, and 304 passengers and crew died, most of them high-school students. As a shocked nation went into mourning, JYP Entertainment knew it was no time to launch a new group, so they quietly postponed their plans. However, the delay had an impact on 6Mix and Cecilia left the company soon afterwards. Some say she had second thoughts about being an idol, others claim she was suffering from a debilitating knee injury, but she returned to China where she now has a successful career as an actor under the name Song Yan-fei.

6Mix was not finished yet, though. JYP Entertainment had plenty of trainees to choose from and Sana, a Japanese trainee already known to the others, was selected to fill the empty spot. Sana had already been placed in an all-Japanese group which was working towards a debut, but her move left them in limbo. Two – Momo and Mina – stayed at JYP Entertainment, but Sika, Riho and Mone soon left (Sika would eventually debut in 2018 with girl group Fanatics). Meanwhile, the new 6Mix line-up began training together through the autumn of 2014.

Somewhere in the JYP Entertainment offices that winter a decision was made to rethink the plans surrounding their first girl group since Miss A in 2010. In February 2015, instead of news of a debut date, K-pop followers learned that a new girl group was to be formed through a TV survival show to be broadcast in the spring. Contestants would all be JYP trainees and would comprise a selection of younger girls who had been working towards a 2017 debut, what was left of the Japanese group and the current members of 6Mix. There would be one notable absentee; sometime in this period, Lena, a lynchpin of the 6Mix concept, left the company, although like Cecilia she would find some future success as an actor in China.

On 10 April 2015, JYP Entertainment dropped a teaser video announcing *Sixteen*, a ten-episode TV survival show on Korean TV channel Mnet. This 'new girl-group project' aimed to whittle down 16 trainees to a seven-girl group. It promised to be revealing – and brutal. JYP was to test what remained of his 6Mix elite against other trainees, to see who had the confidence and talent to perform under immense pressure. The aim was to create a group that had demonstrated their skills and established a fan base ahead of their debut.

The Korean public love talent shows. *Superstar K* had long been popular, but since 2011 *K-pop Star* had eclipsed it by promising the winner a debut with the company of his or her choice. JYP himself had been a judge on all four series of *K-pop Star* and his comments were always incisive yet sensitive. JYP Entertainment had also used the survival show format before to good effect. The 2011 series *Hot Blood Men* had focused on the training of a boy band called One Day. However, before debuting them JYP had split the band into two: 2AM and 2PM. He wasn't afraid to change his mind and had been proved right when both groups went on to great success.

JYP had every hope that this new series would produce an act that would be just as successful. The contenders were the best of his company's female trainees – an older group, who were all around 18, and a younger group, who were 15 or under. They were announced one by one, with their own short teaser, and at last we got to meet the remaining members of 6Mix: Nayeon, whose teaser line 'I am a girl … that is good to date!' made her an instant favourite; ten-year veteran trainee Jihyo; vocal powerhouse Minyoung; bright and bubby Japanese girl Sana; and, the last of the 16 to be revealed, the chic and classy Jeongyeon. In addition, there were two other Japanese trainees: Momo had been training in Korea since April 2012 and had a reputation for being a super-talented dancer, while Mina had only been at JYP for ten months and was a complete unknown, even to keen K-pop followers, who just had her brief but fierce teaser dance to go on.

In the younger group there were three other Korean-born long-term trainees: Dahyun, who was already known to many since a video of her 'eagle dance' in church went viral years earlier; Jiwon, another strong singer who had been a trainee at JYP for three years; and the diminutive rapper Chaeyoung, who, though only just 16 years old, had also been at JYP since 2012.

The other seven trainees were all 15 years old or younger. They were, however, a talented bunch. They included the sisters Chaeryeong (13) and Chaeyeon (14), who had both been signed by JYP after appearing in *K-pop Star 3* in 2013; the sweet, chubby-cheeked Eunsuh (14); Somi (14), a Korean-Canadian with evident star quality whose teaser views made her the second favourite before the show started; and the distinctive Taiwanese Tzuyu (pronounced 'Chewy') who, a month shy of her 16th birthday, had already been at JYP for three years. The youngest of them all, however, was Natty from Thailand, who had just turned 13, but had the confidence and potential to justify her place in the group.

The format of the show pitched competing trainees into fluid major and minor teams, which reflected their chances of eventual success. Majors were given a symbolic pendant, but more importantly a whole set of privileges. They were treated like real idols with luxury dormitories, clothing expenses and daytime access to practice studios. Minors, on the other hand, were treated like poor cousins. Their dorms were cramped and smelly, they had to shop from street markets and, perhaps worst of all, they could only visit the practice studios between nine at night and nine in the morning. This tension drove the show, as a series of challenges allowed minors to prove themselves and take the pendant and the elite place of a major – the decisions were made by JYP after taking viewers' online votes into consideration.

Before the series started in May 2015, JYP revealed that the new girl group would be called Twice – because they would touch people's hearts twice, once through the ears and once through the eyes. *Sixteen* promised surprises and drama, with JYP admitting he had no idea who would make the final group.

The first majors had been selected by his staff based on 'past training scores' and consisted of Nayeon, Minyoung, Jiwon, Momo, Mina, Chaeyoung and Dahyun. There was some surprise that Jeongyeon had been excluded from this elite group, but complete shock that Jihyo had been forced to join the minors (she herself was reduced to tears).

The next ten episodes, aired from May through to July, were devised to assess the girls as potential idols. Singing and dancing were obviously of prime interest, but they were also tested for teamwork, promotion, photoshoots and charisma. As the show progressed fans got to know each of the contestants through fly-on-the-wall clips that accompanied their performances – the nerves, arguments and even jealousies among the girls revealing what a harsh, dog-eat-dog series this was.

In the opening round contestants had to prove they were a star and viewers immediately discovered their favourites, from Dahyun, who reproduced her famous eagle dance, to Sana, who amusingly parodied a cooking show as she made spring rolls for JYP, and 13-year-old Natty, who showcased her skills with a dance she had choreographed herself.

The subsequent photoshoot round brought the chic Jeongyeon, who roller-painted her white t-shirt, and Mina, who wowed the judges by posing as Snow White's Evil Queen, to people's attention. Others felt JYP's ire for failing to charm in front of the camera, but it was Chaeyeon, the older of the Chae sisters, who became the first to be eliminated.

The third round brought the cruellest moments yet: one-against-one battles in which a minor challenged a major for their place. Put on the spot, it was the older trainees' experience that came to the fore. Nayeon impressed with her charisma and stable vocals in a cover of Ariana Grande's 'Santa Tell Me'. Momo put her dance skills on display moving to Ariana's 'Problem' and

Dahyun showed she had more than just a novelty eagle dance with an energetic performance of Pentatonix's 'La La Latch'. Jihyo, back in the majors after a stirring vocal performance in round one, rose to the occasion. The photographer had made pointed remarks about her weight, so Jihyo chose to sing Meghan Trainor's body-positive anthem 'All About That Bass'.

Eunsuh was the next unfortunate trainee to suffer elimination. She clearly had talent, but inexperience and nerves had prevented her showing enough of it. As the halfway mark of the series approached, the majors now consisted of Nayeon, Jeongyeon, Jihyo, Mina, Somi, Chaeryeong and Natty. However, the Taiwanese Tzuyu was winning viewers over with her beauty and a fabulous performance of the Pussycat Dolls' 'Sway' saw her rise to second place in the online vote.

There was no let-up. Next each group was split into two competing teams. The behind-the-scenes footage was illuminating as the teams worked out their choreography, especially when Minyoung and Dahyun went AWOL from practice and temporarily created a serious rift with practice fanatics Tzuyu and Sana. Incredibly, their team's performance of 'Problem' by Ariana was good enough to beat Pharrell's 'Happy', the choice of Nayeon, Jeongyeon, Mina and Chaeryeong.

In the other head-to-head, Jiyho's leadership skills came to the fore as she helmed a team with two non-Korean speakers. Kitted out in red suits and bow-ties, they impressed with 'Uptown Funk' against Momo, Jiwon and Chaeyoung, who covered 'The Way You Love Me' by Keri Hilson, using a table as a prop for some raunchy choreography. The audience plumped for Jihyo's girls, but interestingly in both cases JYP, who reserved particular praise for Jiwon, personally favoured the other team.

The two losing teams now had to compete to see who would be eliminated. To the surprise of many, poor Momo was the victim. She had bewitched many with her dance skills and JYP seemed reluctant to eliminate her, but he said he did so on the basis of her unstable vocals. The others were clearly upset and shocked, and the Japanese girls were almost inconsolable. Had JYP shot himself in the foot by excluding this 'dance machine' from his future girl group?

Next up was something a little more fun. A camping trip meant the girls could all relax – but not too much, because JYP was still watching. After fun games of charades and duelling with plastic hammers while riding giant floaties in the pool, the boss revealed that this, too, was a type of challenge. He explained he was not only looking for great singers and dancers, but also people who did right by others and were true to themselves. To this end, the girls voted for their favourite three fellow contestants. The results were revealing. Virtually all agreed that Jiyho perfectly matched the qualities that JYP highlighted, while Jeongyeon, Minyoung and Nayeon were praised for their helpfulness.

The penultimate challenge again pitted two groups from each team against each other. This time they faced the added task of promoting their performance to attract an audience. Among the highlights were the visit to Nayeon's former high school where she, Jeongyeon and especially Tzuyu (after they gave her some femme fatale tips) completely wowed the schoolboys. The audience were not disappointed as the trio delivered a brilliant cover of Miss A's 'Hush'. When the round was completed, JYP reserved great praise for Chaeyoung's rap in Wonder Girls' 'Nobody', for Jihyo's perfect voice (but not her weight) and for Mina's improved confidence. Sadly, it was Jiwon who walked, JYP clearly believing she had some work to do before debuting.

The final challenge saw majors and minors pitted against each other in full girl-group mode. Each was given a song JYP thought would challenge them and a further number which they would both perform, so a direct comparison could be made. The majors – Chaeyoung, Mina, Minyoung, Natty, Sana and Somi – were mentored by Miss A's Fei and given 'Must be Crazy', a song JYP said requires a keen sense of rhythm, while the minors – Chaeryeong, Dahyun, Jeongyeon, Nayeon, Tzuyu and Jihyo (borrowed from the major team to even up the numbers) – were mentored by 2PM's Jun.K and were tasked with the more vocally challenging 'Truth'.

Both performances were pretty legendary and are often compared favourably with the Twice versions which would soon appear. JYP was pleased with the minor team's performance, picking out the contributions from Jeongyeon and Tzuyu, but once again he also made a point of commending the major team's Chaeyoung. It all came down to the final episode, broadcast on 7 July 2015, as the teams performed back-to-back versions of 'Do It Again'.

Dancing to a brand-new song with set choreography, the girls had to work out the tone and mood for themselves. They had all met up the night before for a watermelon party and it became emotional as they reminisced over both their trainee and *Sixteen* experiences. With so much resting on one final performance, each team played to their strengths. Lacking the vocal power of their opponents, the majors went all out for fun, packing their performance with *aegyo* (cuteness) and acting. In contrast, the minors smashed it vocally with Nayeon, Jeongyeon and Jihyo pulling out all the stops. That didn't escape JYP, who mentioned those three as he gave the minor team his vote. His final decision, however, took into consideration the combined opinions of the live audience, online voters and the JYP staff.

While the audience awaited the final result, the two teams united for the show's theme, 'I'm Gonna Be a Star', before the members who had already been eliminated – Chaeyeon, Eunsuh, Jiwon and Momo – joined them on stage to perform Beyoncé's '7/11'. And then came the moment that the whole series had been building up to – the members of Twice were revealed. The final line-up was to be Nayeon as the show's best vocalist; Jeongyeon, whose talent and enigmatic personality had stood out; Jihyo, who JYP described as 'perfect and ready to debut'; the charismatic and lovable Dahyun; Sana, with her out-there personality and debut-ready skills; and Mina, who JYP Entertainment staff identified as having the most potential. That left Chaeryeong, Minyoung, Natty, Somi and Tzuyu eliminated. Except …

In a series that was filled with shocks and surprises, the biggest was still to come. JYP had decided to add two more members, making a nine- rather than seven-member group. The first addition was Tyuzu, who had featured in the live audience's final seven and topped the online poll. The second was a bigger shock. The JYP staff had unanimously chosen to include Momo, who had been eliminated early in the series. There were shockwaves across the internet as fans discussed the result. Was it fair? Had the audience been cheated? Had it been JYP's intention all along to add members? Opinions differed, but most agreed on one thing. When it came to girl groups, JYP knew what he was doing and he had selected nine girls who were ready to take on the world …

Postscript: What happened to …

The *Sixteen* format required some trainees to be eliminated. It is testament to JYP Entertainment that every one of the contenders gave a good account of themselves and endorsed JYP's claims of wanting good, all-round people at the company. In the event, only four were eliminated as the series progressed – and Momo, of course, was reinstated – but it was still a traumatic experience. JYP promised that those who were eliminated would be given another chance in two years' time, but most of them now realised their dreams of debuting for the company were over.

Chaeryeong

Just 13 when *Sixteen* began, Chaeryeong was probably included to give her experience. However, she impressed with her dancing, singing and charisma, and made it to the end of the series. It was enough for her to stay with the company and it proved a good move for her and JYP Entertainment. In February 2019 she debuted with Itzy, JYP's next girl group. They made quite a splash in Korea, Japan and internationally, and were named Best New Artist at all the major award shows in 2019.

Chaeyeon

The first to be eliminated, Chaeyeon had little chance to show off her talent. She left JYP after the show, but reappeared on another talent show, *Produce 48*, in 2018, and came 12th. As a result, she debuted in the 12-member girl group Iz*One in October 2018. The group established themselves as a successful group in Korea and Japan, with their 2020 comeback album *Bloom*Iz* charting well in both countries.

Eunsuh

Only 14, Eunsuh struggled to progress from her initial cute image, and when she made an obvious mistake in her choreography in the one-to-one challenge, her time on *Sixteen* was up.

She tried again on the 2017 talent show *Idol School*, but still failed to make the final group.

Jiwon

A strong singer, many believed Jiwon had a good chance of succeeding on *Sixteen*, but nerves seemed to get the better of her. She was the last to be eliminated, with JYP citing her off-beat dancing and unstable vocals as the reason for letting her go. In 2017, she, too, entered *Idol School* and came sixth, which led to her joining Fromis_9, who debuted in January 2018. Their early releases made the top five in Korea, and in 2018 and 2019 the group were nominated for several new artist awards.

Minyoung

Poor Minyoung. Was it just never meant to be? Her dream of debuting with 6Mix evaporated, but she was given a second chance on *Sixteen*. It seemed a formality that her strong vocals and experience would see her make it into Twice, but the pressure of the show seemed to affect her. Minyoung failed to establish herself as a major player with the viewers or JYP and she missed out again. After *Sixteen*, Minyoung gave up the idea of debuting and returned to her studies.

Natty

The youngest of all the *Sixteen* contestants, Natty collected many fans as the series progressed with her energy, personality and no little talent, especially as a dancer. After the show, Natty left JYP and she, too, tried her luck on *Idol School* in 2017. She made it to the last round, but again ultimately missed the cut. Still young and popular in Thailand, Natty has time on her side and in April 2020 signed with Swing Entertainment, with the intention of debuting as a solo artist.

Somi

Somi was unlucky not to make the final Twice line-up, having spent most of the series in the major team. JYP sensed she had star quality but suggested she needed a little more time before debuting. He was right. In 2016 she represented JYP in the first season of the talent show *Produce 101* and won, becoming a member of girl group I.O.I. They debuted in May 2016 and made a strong impact, but they disbanded after little more than six months together. Somi continued to raise her profile hosting TV variety shows but held on to her musical ambitions. In 2019 she left JYP Entertainment for rival company YG to pursue a solo career.

2

DEBUT

No matter the discussions on the fairness of *Sixteen* – JYP Entertainment felt the necessity to make an official statement the day after the show's finale to clarify what had happened. JYP had spoken. Momo and Tzuyu had been added to the seven successful trainees selected by the audience and staff and would take their places in Twice. While everyone had their favourites, and some were disappointed to see certain trainees fail to make the group, it was generally agreed that JYP had ended up with a selection that complemented each other and contained a mix of proven talent and enormous potential. Whether it was luck or judgement, JYP had landed on nine girls who, between them, ticked all the boxes.

The group was well balanced in age, with Nayeon the oldest at 20; the 96-liners (those born in 1996), Jeongyeon, Momo and Sana, were all still 19 years old; the 97-liners, Jihyo and Mina, were 18; and Dahyun was 17. That left the 16-year-olds, Chaeyoung and the group's youngest member, Tzuyu. Known in Korea as the *maknae*, the youngest had special dispensation to be extra cute and not carry any responsibilities especially in a

K-pop group. Although five of the group were Korean, Mina, Momo and Sana were from Japan and Tzuyu was from Taiwan – ideal for building on the *hallyu* or Korean Wave – the rise in interest in Korean culture in East Asia.

They were also varied in personality. Jihyo was sensible and caring, a natural leader; the group's extrovert, Dahyun, was goofy and naturally funny; and Nayeon seemed to be eternally cheerful and, despite being the oldest, eager to mess around and have fun. Jeongyeon had her chic image to preserve, but liked to tease the others, while Sana managed to be witty and cute at the same time. The others – especially Mina – were more reserved, but fans who had watched *Sixteen* knew that Tzuyu had a wicked sense of humour which was bound to emerge sooner or later. These were early days and when they weren't performing the girls, especially the younger members, were understandably shy in front of the cameras.

Sixteen had given the audience a good indication of what each individual excelled at and what they might offer Twice. In a group with a large number of members it was expected that some would have specific roles, as well as performing the choreography together. Jeongyeon, Jihyo and Nayeon had the confidence and vocal stability to be the lead vocalists; Mina and Momo had displayed incredible dance skills; Chaeyoung and Dahyun were clearly the designated rappers; and Sana and Tzuyu's dance and vocal skills had come on in leaps and bounds during the series.

The girls had no time to recover from *Sixteen*. They went straight from the show into rehearsals for their first releases as Twice. As is common for any K-pop group, all nine of them soon moved into a dorm in the South Korean capital, Seoul, where they would live together. At least it was a ground-floor flat and the house next door was empty, so it wasn't such a problem that they were sometimes a noisy bunch. They sorted out who would room with who with little fuss. The youngsters, Chaeyoung, Dahyun and Tzuyu, took one room; Jihyo, Mina, Nayeon and Sana shared the large room; while best friends Jeongyeon and Momo took the final room.

Like any new roommates they soon began to discover each other's habits – good and bad. Chaeyoung fell asleep instantly and could sleep forever. Nayeon not only talked in her sleep but also slept with her eyes wide open. Mina liked staying in bed whether she was sleeping or not, while Tzuyu was the early riser who could be relied upon to get the others up. Meanwhile, Jeongyeon and Momo, who shared a bed in their room (separated by Momo's huge teddy bear), became known as 'the married couple'. Surprisingly, it was the cool-looking Jeongyeon who became the 'mother' of the group, cleaning and tidying the flat and chivvying the others to do their share of the chores.

JYP needed to reveal his new group to the world before people moved on to the next survival show or lost interest in their favourites from *Sixteen*. This gave the girls little time to rehearse and record the new material, to learn and master the choreography to the songs, and to shoot the all-important music video. The girls were expected to look their best for their first appearance, so many of them were on strict diets. However, they were practising so hard that they were losing weight anyway. Momo, who surprised them all with the amount she ate, still managed to lose seven kilos in this hectic period. Everything had to be perfect before Twice made their debut – one of the most important dates in the career of any K-pop artist.

Through July and into August, the members appeared on *Twice TV*, a short, five-part series shown on V LIVE. The first four episodes profiled each of the girls as they talked about their journey so far, while the last episode featured them all having a meal with JYP. He said he liked to take all his acts to dinner as he worries about them, especially the girl groups. He explained that he expects JYP Entertainment artists to strive to become better people and he read out letters from each of the members of Twice, revealing how they felt about debuting. He reassured them that if they worked as hard and performed as well as they had promised in their letters, they would become the best group in the world.

He also asked them to vote for the leader of Twice. He said a leader must put themselves last for the sake of the group; represent the group in discussions with the company staff; and set an example to other members, sorting any issues that arise. After the meal the members voted for Jihyo to be their leader, with Jeongyeon receiving the second-highest number of votes.

A K-pop act only gets one chance to debut – the moment of the unveiling of the artist or group, an opportunity to make a big splash. The pop world is ready to be impressed, eager to spot the next big thing and generally looks favourably on nervous young artists stepping into the limelight for the first time. If the debutantes can create a good first impression, their careers are off to a flying start and everything is easy and exciting. If they flop, they face an uphill battle. It's not impossible to come back after bombing on a debut, but those who have managed it are few and far between.

A successful debut launches the act into the collective pop consciousness. It communicates the concept and image of a group or singer as simply as possible to attract as many fans as possible. It probably won't top the charts or set any streaming records, as it's difficult to compete with existing acts, but hopefully it will make a big enough impact to be noted by Korean and international K-pop fans.

How an act debuts depends on the strategy and budget of their company. Debut day for artists with great ambition will involve a live showcase in front of an invited audience of lucky fans and a question-and-answer session with the media – the whole thing may even be livestreamed for fans across the world to watch. The act will then be expected to perform their debut single (and sometimes other songs) on one or more of the weekly Korean TV music shows. There is a show broadcast most days, with the most influential being *M Countdown, Show! Music Core, Inkigayo, Music Bank, Show Champion* and *The Show*. These are all incredibly popular and performances will often appear on YouTube for repeated viewing. There they will join the debut music video, which is another massive opportunity to impress new fans.

The great K-pop girl groups in whose footsteps Twice were hoping to follow all had explosive debuts. Major company SM's Girls' Generation's 2007 debut 'Into the New World' was an anthemic and high-energy song that went to number five in Korea. In 2009 the term 'monster rookies' was invented for YG Entertainment's 2NE1, after twin videos of their fun and catchy debut 'Fire' received a million views in a day. JYP's own Miss A's iconic 2010 debut 'Bad Girl, Good Girl' was a great showcase, and, just a year before Twice prepared to debut, Red Velvet (SM again) had demonstrated debuts could achieve international success when 'Happiness' went to number four in *Billboard*'s World Digital charts. The bar had been set pretty high.

These groups were all still active (although 2NE1 were on a semi-hiatus) as Twice prepared to debut and there were other new girl groups keen to steal their thunder. Wanna B debuted in July 2015, April in August and DIA were unveiled in September, while Lovelyz, CLC, Mamamoo and GFriend had all debuted successfully in the past year. It was a crowded market.

Sixteen had given Twice an advantage. It was a tremendously popular show and all the girls had each picked up a number of fans. Whereas lots of groups head into their debuts from a standing start, K-pop fans already knew who Twice were. On 7 October 2015 JYP Entertainment launched the band's official website and announced that the group would debut with a mini-album. Over the next two weeks there were a series of teasers – photos and short videos – that helped fans become more familiar with the members.

The main image of the group featured them in a line, all with hands on hips, staring intently at the lens like they meant business. Dressed in variations of red, black and camouflage they looked fresh and edgy in an assortment of graphic-embellished and lace-fringed crop tops, short skirts and shorts, plenty of wrist straps and bangles, and black platform boots. Nayeon, the only one wearing fishnet hold-ups, took centre position, flanked by Sana and Jeongyeon. The latter still had her short hair, but had dyed it rose pink, while Momo, at the left end of the line, was now sporting striking blonde locks.

Each of the girls was individually photographed in their teaser outfit (that *Sixteen* challenge had paid dividends!) and fans were able to get a closer look. Sana looked stunning as she crouched with her finger on her lips and her hair tied up in two fun bunches. Tzuyu, her dark hair falling over one eye, looked intriguing as she bit her lip, while a slightly mournful Jihyo showed off her new auburn hair. The others looked slightly awkward, but they had plenty of time to get that right, and it didn't matter anyway because the outfits and make-up were perfect.

Each of the girls also had a 20-second video teaser in which a zombie intruder interrupted them as they were doing an ordinary activity. The humorous twist was that the girls were totally unfazed by the intrusion. Among fans the favourite was Dahyun's teaser, which had her dancing alone in her living room. As she starts her now-famous eagle dance, two zombies materialise and, of course, they can't resist joining in. Another popular clip featured Jeongyeon, clearly being cast as the group's edgy member. She is sitting on the sofa watching TV and eating popcorn when her zombie appears. She tries feeding him some popcorn, but when he spits it out she gives him a taste of his own medicine, screaming and scaring the living daylights out of him!

For the nine members of Twice, 20 October must have come around so quickly. It had been a whirlwind six months for them, but they had been well prepared by the company and been given advice on what to expect by members of Miss A and second-generation group Wonder Girls. The day would not only see the release of their debut mini-album and single, but also their showcase at Uniqlo Ax Hall in Seoul, where they would perform on stage in front of the fans for the first time. If that wasn't enough to set the nerves on edge, it would also be broadcast live on V LIVE.

Park Jin-young had come up with a new genre to describe Twice's music. He called it colour pop, a fresh sound forged from a combination of rock, R'n'B and hip-hop, with infectious if unconventional lyrics. Many waited to hear their debut single to decide if colour pop was a real thing or simply JYP Entertainment promoting its new act. The title, 'Like Ooh Ahh', certainly contained a promise of fun and exuberance.

Perhaps the biggest surprise was that Twice were not going to debut with one of JYP's songs. He was a prolific writer and had penned songs for g.o.d, Rain, 2PM, Wonder Girls, Got7, Miss A and even for Western artists such as Will Smith. However, JYP often leaned on retro influences in his songs so, determined to create a fresh sound for his new group's debut single, he turned to an emerging production team who had already begun to make waves.

They were called Black Eyed Pilseung (which translates as Black Eyed Victory), a clever Korean take on will.i.am's group Black Eyed Peas. Black Eyed Pilseung were a duo made up of Rado and Choi Kyu-sung. Under his real name, Song Joo-young, Rado had debuted with boy band Someday in 2009 before moving behind the controls to work on hits for 4minute, Apink and Trouble Maker, while Choi Kyu-sung was building a reputation having produced hits for T-ara, Beast and Hyuna. Forming Black Eyed Pilseung in 2014, they were behind 'Touch my Body', a number one in Korea for girl group Sistar, and 'Missing' a top-ten hit for boy band Teen Top. They had then worked for JYP Entertainment on songs for Miss A and Got7, and JYP was convinced they were the ideal team to create colour pop.

It was nearly time. The music video was due to drop at midnight on 19 October, and to welcome it the girls held a pyjama party in their dorm at 11.30 p.m., broadcast on V LIVE. Snuggled up on their sofa, each hugging their plushies, they talked about life in the dorm together and their midnight feasts and dance parties. As midnight approached, despite saying they were nervous, they became more and more excited and high-spirited. When the song was finally revealed they were elated, singing and dancing along – all except for Jeongyeon, for whom the moment was too much. She burst into tears.

It must have been hard for the excited girls to sleep, but the next day was debut day, their showcase and their first live performance of 'Like Ooh Ahh'. At the concert hall, they fulfilled all the fans' expectations. Looking superb in their red and camouflaged outfits, they came across as individuals and as a synchronised group with energetic choreography and vocals that didn't miss a beat. There was only one moment that didn't go to plan. As Jihyo's first line arrived, she was overcome with emotion and started to cry. She had waited ten long years for this moment and fans immediately realised what this meant to her.

Now we discovered what colour pop was. It was an updated version of the bubblegum sound. It was fun, upbeat and sing-along. It had a super-sweet feel, too, but that was cleverly under-cut with changes of pace. It was, however, distinctly third-generation K-pop, with its driving beat, rap parts, the R'n'B feel of the verses and the effortless integration of clap-ping, rock guitar and synth sounds. Even a flute was made to seem a natural part of the instrumental. Jiyho and Nayeon had the lion's share of the vocal lines with Chaeyoung and Dahyun taking the small rap part. Not that the others didn't contribute; chiming in with alternate lines, they added a 'girls together' vibe, bringing humour and spikiness to the number.

The song itself, with lyrics from relatively new writer Sam Lewis, focused on the girls' desire to fall in love – but not with guys who are only interested in them because they're pretty. It introduced Twice as modern girls who knew how attractive they were and that they didn't have to settle for second best. It wasn't exactly girl crush, but it had plenty of elements of that inde-pendent spirit.

The showcase also saw Twice present other songs from the mini-album. They performed the ballad 'Like a Fool', a difficult song to sing on your debut. Nerves clearly got to some, with Jeongyeon and Sana suffering more than most. In fact, Sana was visibly upset after failing to reach a high note on one of her lines. However, the stability of Jiyho, Mina and Nayeon helped them pull through, and as the song progressed they all grew stronger. They were much more confident tackling three of the songs which had featured in the *Sixteen* finale: the mid-tempo 'Truth' brought a kaleidoscope choreography that made the most of the nine-member group; with a more R'n'B vibe, 'Must Be Crazy' allowed them to let loose and have fun; and they turned 'Do it Again' into a hair-flipping, high-energy party with Momo taking centre stage – there were plaudits for her fantastic dance moves and for pulling off a rap part as well.

Online, the reaction to the showcase was positive. Fans were gobsmacked at how pretty every single member of Twice was, declaring them the best-looking girl group ever! Others noted the freshness of their image and sound. And JYP Entertainment certainly seemed to have succeeded in overcoming one major hurdle: with so many girls in a group, how do you make each of them distinctive? Fans could pick each one out by their hair or their outfit and revelled in the girls' individuality. Twice had arrived – and in some style.

3

THE STORY BEGINS

On the same day as their showcase, Twice had released their video for 'Like Ooh Ahh'. A YouTube music video was an essential device to reach out to fans, especially international fans. The global availability of YouTube ensured that the excited and the curious living outside South Korea – from the USA and Europe to the Middle East and especially in Japan and other parts of Asia – could see what the fuss over JYP's new girl group was all about.

The music video had developed into the major tool for promoting an artist. An entertaining, interesting or visually appealing video could gain millions of views and significantly boost an act's profile. The pressure to produce a captivating video that bore repeated viewing for Twice's debut single was therefore immense.

Responsibility for producing the video was given to Naïve Productions, a company that had worked with all JYP's major acts, including Miss A and Got7. Their job was to communicate Twice's concept – fresh, colourful and fun – and introduce the members to a global audience. With Halloween approaching, they opted to surround the girls with zombies (explaining why the undead had co-starred in the girls' teasers) to add humour and excitement.

The video begins with a single-take shot as the camera pans around an abandoned school to introduce each of the members. The grey background contrasts with the sharpness of the girls' high-school-styled outfits, among them Nayeon in a short yellow-and-black tartan skirt, Sana in a cheerleader dress and Jiyho in gym gear, with the full school uniform given to youngest member Tzuyu. The second section finds them back in their debut outfits with the full nine performing the song's choreography on the roof at dusk in front of baying, fenced-off zombies. This is intercut with their escape on the school bus, which, for some reason, takes them to a fairground for the final scene. There they dance with the zombies, pacifying them by showing them how to have some fun.

It is a simple plot, very loosely related to the song's lyrics – at least if the zombies represent those guys who want the girls' attention just because they're so attractive. However, it is incredibly effective. It matches the energy and upbeat feeling of the song and, of course, the Twice members look fantastic. Equally importantly, they look unique, with fans now able to pick out their favourites – and not just the obvious red-haired Jiyho or Jeongyeon with her pink bob. There's Dahyun with her red highlights, Chaeyoung with her side-parted, shoulder-length hair or the unmistakable long legs of Tzuyu.

The video also communicates another vital element of Twice: these girls like to have fun. From Nayeon's beguiling wink at the opening to Sana's self-mocking failure to imitate Mina and Momo's balletic poses, to the bonus finale with clips of each of them dancing in the aisle on the bus, if producers Naïve had set out to charm viewers they had totally succeeded. Beautiful, vivacious and just a little quirky – who wouldn't be eager to find out more about Twice?

Confirmation that the video had pushed all the right buttons came almost immediately. Within 24 hours 'Like Ooh Ahh' had been viewed over a million times and that total doubled after two days. Among K-pop videos only solo singer Taeyeon's 'I' was more popular around the globe. Their video wasn't breaking any records (yet), but Twice were most definitely on the world map.

Meanwhile the mini-album, *The Story Begins*, had dropped. Lasting just over 20 minutes it contained six tracks: 'Like Ooh Ahh' and the other songs performed at the showcase – 'Do it Again', 'Going Crazy', 'Truth' and 'Like a Fool' – as well as the yet-to-be-performed live 'Candy Boy'. Aside from the ballad 'Like a Fool' (in which the vocals, in contrast to their showcase version, are spot on and moving), the up-tempo, good vibes and high-energy concept were maintained throughout, but the sound mined a host of genres – hip-hop, funk, R'n'B and EDM – so it was hard to classify. Perhaps it was colour pop!

Both the single and the mini-album made an instant impression on the charts. *The Story Begins* went straight to number four on South Korea's Gaon Album Chart and 'Like Ooh Ahh' debuted in the charts at number 22. Both also registered on the *Billboard* World charts and in Japanese charts. For Twice, though, this was just the start. The hard work now began with promoting the single. This meant more nerve-racking performances for the novice members and an exhausting schedule of early morning make-up sessions, endless rehearsals, tense recordings and hours of sitting backstage waiting to be called.

The first of these performances – known as 'debut stages' – took place two days after the showcase, on the Mnet channel's weekly pop programme *M Countdown*. Years later fans would marvel at the one girl chanting on her own as their performance commenced. It's hard to imagine now, but their fan base was minuscule compared to the established acts on the show. *M Countdown* had given them a Halloween set, but there were no zombies here, just nine girls giving their all on the dancefloor and singing live. They had swapped the debut outfits for a mostly black and grey look that still maintained the cute but sexy concept. Jihyo stood out in her 'After Dark' t-shirt and hold-ups, while Momo took viewers' breath away in her cut-off denim shorts and tight crop top.

As was often the case on the music shows, Twice also performed a second song, 'Do it Again', on *M Countdown*. They re-emerged in fetching red, blue and black athleisure outfits (very much on trend in autumn 2015). This time the choreography was completely girly, full of skips and jumps, while the performance was marked by rapping from Chaeyoung and Momo, with Sana left alone on stage at the end to show some top *aegyo*. Some fans were now beginning to wonder, were Twice going to be a cutesy girl group or a more edgy girl-crush group?

Over the next week they repeated their exertions on *Music Bank*, *Show! Music Core*, *Inkigayo* and *The Show*. Each time they seemed more relaxed and confident about singing live (many acts, especially rookie groups, lip sync on these shows). They also appeared in different outfits each time. Generally, they wore crop tops and tight or flared skirts or shorts (Jeongyeon's somehow being shorter than the others'!). None of them wore the same outfit, but there was always a colour or pattern that gave them a group identity. On *Show! Music Core*, for example, where there was a yellow and black theme, Mina and Chaeyoung wore yellow-and-black-check crop tops, Tzuyu and Dahyun wore flared yellow, white and black patterned skirts, and Sana had the same pattern on a dress.

Audiences were amazed at just how good they all looked. They were used to K-pop groups having one or two 'visual' members who were noted for their looks, but with Twice it was impossible to see who that was – they were all equally beautiful. Fans would pick their 'bias' – their favourite member – then change their mind after the next show. The 'bias-wreckers' – members who would make fans question their choice – were often Mina, Momo, Dahyun or Jeongyeon, but every single member was guaranteed a mention in discussion forums.

The next thing fans noted was the choreography. Devised by renowned K-pop choreographer Lia Kim, it utilised all nine girls in a series of fun dance moves. Fans attempting to do the dances themselves soon discovered that they were not quite as complicated as they looked (although Twice were dancing in high heels!) and once they had mastered the flute playing, the making a heart with their hands, the throwing kisses, the Marilyn Monroe holding her skirt move, the 'ooh ahh' leg twist and the jumps and shakes, it all came together. The breakdown wasn't quite so easy to imitate, though. Momo was a class act and her neck-jerking, hair-flicking solo dance was the work of a professional.

Music shows were only the half of it. The six weeks of promotion were filled with magazine interviews and photoshoots, fan signings, live radio shows and recorded TV broadcasts. For the nine members of Twice, who just five months previously had still been trainees, this was all very novel. The evening before their *M Countdown* debut they took part in a photoshoot for *Elle* – their first magazine shoot. One set of pictures was taken on a sports field after nightfall. The girls were cold, but excited, and came across as a group with boundless energy. Another set of pictures was taken in a studio and these shots were exquisite. Dressed in shiny black and lace, the girls exuded a femme-fatale vibe and posed like born models – they had come a long way since the *Sixteen* photoshoot challenge.

Fan meetings were another new phenomenon for the fledgling group. K-pop acts were expected to meet their supporters, and outside the studio after their debut stage over 200 people sat patiently waiting for them. The girls emerged wrapped in blankets, waved and each said a few slightly awkward words to the assembled fans. They looked visibly shocked at how many had turned up. It was enough to bring Sana to tears, but the numbers were only going to get bigger.

The new fans were overjoyed to discover there was a second series of *Twice TV* to coincide with their debut. Running weekly until Christmas, the episodes documented what the group had been getting up to, including photo sessions for the album, behind the scenes at their debut stage, the *Elle* magazine photoshoot and the filming of their first commercial – for a school uniform brand called Skoolooks. With later episodes following them to the zoo and the fairground rides at Everland, South Korea's largest theme park, viewers were able to see them at work and at play.

Some episodes were pure fun, especially the parody of *Sixteen* which opened the series. Each of the girls played another member, except for Momo, who was excellent in the role of Park Jin-young. Nayeon was hilarious as Sana and Mina took her impression of Tzuyu as far as it could go. In episode five they wrote their own profiles and showed off their individual skills, including Nayeon's girl-crush pose and Sana's massage skills. In another episode the challenge was to make a 15-second film. Mina's suggestion of a ghost film was voted the best (ahead of Momo's idea of a commercial for pigs' trotters!) and the result was genuinely scary, especially Tzuyu pulling an eyeball-less stare.

Fans loved the *Twice TV* series, but what people really wanted to see was Twice on television and in particular on variety shows. The South Koreans love their variety shows and have so many to choose from. Some are straightforward chat shows, but the favourites challenge guests in order to reveal different facets of their personalities. The challenges can be silly and fun or tough and testing, and the hosts are always ready to tease and mock the guests, however big a star they might be.

Twice's very first variety show was on YouTube channel Kthe1's *Let's Dance*, and they announced themselves with their chant. Like many K-pop groups, Twice had their own greeting, which translates as 'One in a million – hello we are Twice', and they had spent the summer rehearsing it. The show required the girls to play some simple games to decide which duo got to teach the mystery man, who wore black and a motorcycle crash helmet, different elements of the 'Like Ooh Aah' choreography. Perhaps unsurprisingly, Dahyun and Jihyo won the loudest voice challenge, while Nayeon and Tzuyu triumphed in the dance challenge, in which they had to remember the choreography for random hits. If this was a test, they passed with flying colours, showing they could be funny, cute and talented, often all at the same time.

What fans were really waiting for was an appearance on *Weekly Idol*, one of the longest-running and most popular of all the variety shows. The 60-minute show poked fun at its guests, while giving them a chance to show fans their true personalities. It had launched so many K-pop acts on the journey to stardom and the fact that Twice had debuted a mere 50 days before being invited onto the show was an indication of the impact they had made with 'Like Ooh Ahh'.

The show was hosted by popular TV personality Defconn and Sungkyu from boy band Infinite. He was only MCing for his second week, after the departure of regular host Jeong Hyeong-don, and it was perhaps his nervousness that helped Twice feel more confident, because rather than the timid young girls that viewers might have expected to see, they were buzzing with energy and personality, and great entertainment value.

The show begins with *Weekly Idol* introductions, where each member of the group introduces themselves through their nick-name. Some of the descriptions were obvious: Mina, who had trained as a ballet dancer, was the Black Swan Ballerina; Tzuyu the Tall *Maknae*; Sana was Cutie-Sexy; and Nayeon Bright Energy. Others needed a little explanation. Dahyun called herself Energetic Tofu, because her skin was pale like tofu; Momo was Performance and Belly, not because she liked revealing her abs, but on account of her insatiable appetite; and Jiyho was the Mic, because she didn't need a microphone as her voice was so loud. That left the besties, Chaeyoung and Jeongyeon. They had picked up a reputation as the No Jam (or No Fun) Brothers, because they often laughed at jokes that the others just didn't get.

The main segment of the show, called Idol of the Week, set the guests challenges from a menu of games designed to demon-strate their talents or charisma. As first-timers on the show, Twice avoided some of the difficult tasks, such as dancing the choreog-raphy from a random selection of their songs at double speed or performing the choreography of one hit to a different song. What they did get was dancing another group's choreography. It was something they would have done many times for fun or in practice as trainees, but remembering the moves on prime-time TV could be difficult – not for dance machine Momo, though, who was up straightaway to EXO's 'Call Me Baby', or Nayeon, who had no trouble recalling the moves to AoA's 'Heart Attack'. By the time Miss A's 'Display' came on, virtually all of them took to the dancefloor. Only Nayeon stayed seated and she came to life for the final track, 'Bad', dancing with host Sungkyu, who had sung on the original hit.

Twice had gone on *Weekly Idol* to introduce themselves to the Korean public (and international fans who caught the episode later on YouTube). They wanted to present an image of beauty and energy. The first of these was easy. Even though they were dressed down for the show in jumpers, jeans and comfortable skirts, they still looked gorgeous. The second was more difficult, but they rose to the occasion in the Crazy Dance challenge. Just required to go crazy to 'Like Ooh Ahh', they did it with style and humour. Tzuyu stole Dahyun's eagle dance; Jihyo fizzed around the stage brilliantly; Momo displayed her breakdancing skills; and Dahyun became a hair-flicking, arm-flinging blur who didn't stop even when the music finished. For all their efforts, Jeongyeon was pronounced the winner for her lolloping and crouching dance, which had the other members in hysterics. How could they possibly say she was no fun?

Finally, they had to take on the special talents round. It was one thing to claim you had a skill, but proving it in front of the cameras was something else. Poor Jeongyeon was quickly brought down to earth when she was asked to prove she could play the buk drum, a traditional Korean percussion instrument. Although she clearly knew how to play it, the hosts jokingly mocked her skills. Tzuyu demonstrated that she excelled at pulling model poses, only for Jiyho and Jeongyeon to pull their own poses – to everyone's amusement. The real stars of the round, though, were Chaeyoung, whose caricature drawing of the hosts was very impressive, and Sana, who displayed her calligraphy skills, even creating a poster declaiming the slogan, 'No Sana, No Life'. In Korean *sana* means 'to live' and fans had quickly adopted the phrase.

Weekly Idol rounded off a successful if not sensational debut for JYP's new girl group. After some initial success, 'Like Ooh Aah' had fallen in the charts but was increasingly looking like a sleeper hit – a release that remains in the charts, gradually becoming more and more popular. In November, the single had started to climb the charts again, reaching number nine, despite tough competition. Meanwhile, in the Philippines, Japan, Taiwan and other Asian countries, international K-pop fans were picking up on Twice. On 14 November, the music video for 'Like Ooh Aah' passed ten million YouTube views. To mark this pretty amazing achievement, JYP dropped Twice Special Video 'C', which showed the girls, in their original video high-school outfits, performing the whole dance in the dilapidated schoolroom.

Over 50 days the smiles and copiable dances of the Twice girls had caught the attention of many K-pop lovers, and the infectious melodies and chorus of 'Like Ooh Aah' had been played on radio, TV and in shops across Korea and beyond. They had already begun to fulfil JYP's mission to captivate fans twice, through the eyes and through the ears, but their story had only just begun …

4

ONCE

K-pop fans are among the most passionate in the world. Sure, the West has witnessed the mass devotion of Beliebers or Directioners, but nothing on the scale of K-pop fandoms. Having a network of thousands who eagerly await every release and show is essential to an act's success in K-pop, and the fandom is a cherished and nurtured body.

Being a K-pop fan is often an active as well as a passive activity. These fans do not only follow their idols, listen to their recordings, read or watch interviews and attend fan meetings, they actively play a part in promoting them. They might stream the music videos to increase the number of views, vote for the act on award shows or collectively lobby radio or TV stations to feature their favourites. Many, although understanding and respecting that their idols are people too, feel a deep relationship with a group or particular idol and it is a feeling that is often reciprocated by the stars, who feel nourished by the love they receive.

The growing Twice fandom already had their own nickname for Twice, calling them 'Teudoongie' – a word combining *Teu*, the first syllable of Twice in Korean, and *doongi*, a word meaning cutie – but what they really wanted was an official name for their fandom. K-pop fan-club names are usually a little more creative than Little Mix's Mixers. BTS have Army, Blackpink have Blink, while some are even more imaginative – take TVXQ's Cassiopeia or Seventeen's Carat. On 4 November 2015, Twice released their official fandom name through their Instagram account. JYP Entertainment had approved the idea that Jiyho had floated in the debut countdown V LIVE broadcast: Twice fans were to be known as 'Once'.

The Instagram message read, 'A lot of fans liked "Once". Once and Twice. Once then Twice. They seem to go together. If you love us even Once we'll repay you with Twice our love. It's difficult to connect with people and getting people to love is the most difficult of all. We'll work hard so that you can look at us Once and fall in love with us Twice. Be with us until the end. We love you.'

Twice's early fans took to the name immediately. It brought them together as a fandom and enabled them to meet each other and talk about the group. The main forum for this was online fan cafés. Fan cafés are an important part of K-pop culture as they give fans an opportunity to gather information about new releases, fan meetings or sightings of idols, and to voice their own opinions on the act. Occasionally members of the group themselves even post on the sites, but unfortunately, as they're generally conducted in Korean, they are of limited value to international fans.

The fan cafés of successful groups might amass over 200,000 members, but a group just establishing themselves, as Twice was in late 2015, might have around 25,000. However, this is still enough to mobilise support for a group and, with the award season approaching, Once had arrived just in time. As a fandom they could encourage fans to vote for Twice and for those attending the ceremonies to be loud in their support for the girls.

Award shows are a high point in the K-pop calendar, with companies, acts and fans alike determined to make an impression. Winning an award is an important recognition of achievement and a place in the K-pop firmament is determined as much by awards won as chart hits, record sales or arena tours. There are many awards available, ranging from the single of the year to the best overall and global acts. *Bonsangs* are prizes awarded to up to a dozen acts who have excelled in certain categories, but the most cherished awards are the *daesangs*, which are special prizes reserved for the very top groups or artists.

For such a new group as Twice, the only prize they had any real chance of winning was a newcomer award. Generally speaking, until 18 months or even two years have passed since their debut, groups are termed 'rookie acts'. However, even within this, group competition can be fierce. Twice had only debuted a month or so before the award season began and were competing against groups such as CLC, who already had two top ten EPs, Lovelyz, who had released three charting singles, and GFriend, who had debuted back in January and were seriously popular. Even if they didn't take home a trophy, though, attending and being seen with established K-pop idols was a prize in itself, and if they performed at the ceremony it would give a real boost to their status in the industry.

In early November, Twice lost out to GFriend at the Melon Music Awards (MMAs), but – amazingly – at the Mnet Asian Music Awards (MAMAs), which took place in Hong Kong in early December, they were nominated for the Artist of the Year award. Realistically, they had no chance of winning, with K-pop giants EXO, Big Bang and Girls' Generation all in contention.

However, the Rookie of the Year award, decided by votes on the MAMAs website, was firmly in their sights – as long as Once rallied to the cause.

It was Twice's first awards show and they were determined to enjoy it, hanging out with their JYP Entertainment friends Got7, who were performing. JYP himself also took to the stage for a medley of songs, including a dance he performed with a female dancer to 'Who's Your Mama?'. Standing up and dancing, the Twice girls did their best to support the boss, but when the dance got a little too suggestive some of them just couldn't watch, hiding their face behind their hands in embarrassment.

Fortunately, they had recovered by the time they took to the stage to receive the Best New Artist – Female award, their first ever trophy. The girls were dressed smartly, mainly in black jackets and skirts, but what grabbed the attention were some dramatic hair colour changes: Tzuyu's long straight hair was now a crimson-red, Chaeyoung's shorter hair was a dark blue and Sana's locks were a beautiful dark pink.

While Nayeon jumped forward to collect their award, as Twice's leader it was Jiyho's responsibility to give the group's acceptance speech. She might have told the audience that she was nervous, but she spoke like she had been picking up awards for years. She thanked Park Jin-young, who was now sitting in the audience with a smile a mile wide, gave the first official call-out to Once and modestly insisted that Twice still had much to improve upon, promising that they would work hard to become better people and performers.

As they reached two months since debut and approached their first Christmas together as a group, Twice announced a special gift for Once. On 21 December they uploaded three cover videos of JYP classics. One was a dance video set to 2PM's 'ADTOY' ('All Day I Think of You'). Featuring Momo,

Chaeyoung, Jeongyeon, Sana and Tzuyu, dressed identically in long white shirts and short black shorts, it takes place in a flood-lit night-time garden. With a choreography based around five chairs, the five members perform a highly synchronised dance that alternates between cute and seductive.

Meanwhile, in the second video the other four members – Dahyun, Jiyho, Mina and Nayeon – were indoors in a room decorated for Christmas. Dahyun was at the piano, Jiyho stood next to her like a soloist and the others perched on the sofa as they performed a cover of Wonder Girls' 2011 hit 'Be My Baby'. While Dahyun surprised many with her piano-playing ability, Jiyho's confident and stable lead vocal was just as Once had learned to expect, and Nayeon's soft tones and Mina's sweet, almost angelic, voice complemented beautifully.

The trio of covers was completed by a whole-group effort in which they sang Got7's 'Confession Song' from 2014. This was cute and fun Twice in their Christmas jumpers, standing around the Christmas tree, playing with the balloons and preparing party treats. Impressively, Chaeyoung and Dahyun added a rap which they wrote themselves, but Dahyun earned the most laughs for singing the 'Hajima' line at the beginning. It was a line from another Got7 single, 'Stop, Stop It', and Dahyun had had a lead role in the music video. Once appreciated the reference.

Christmas in K-popland means TV specials, and with Twice's appealing visuals and feelgood vibes they were much in demand. They recorded two performances for the *Music Bank* special that was broadcast on Christmas Day. One was a new version of 'Like Ooh Aah' with additional choreography elements, while the other was a cover of a 1997 hit by Baby V.O.X. called 'YaYaYa'. Kitted out in pink and white fluffy woollen tops and A-line skirts, this was as girly as Twice had so far been seen. Tzuyu's voice really shone in the sugary sweet song, but the concept surprised some Onces: this image wasn't what they expected of the group.

Before the year ended, Twice were able to tick off another K-pop tradition. They participated in the SBS (Seoul Broadcasting System) Christmas special *Gayo Daejun*, which has been a Korean TV festive favourite since 1997. Originally an awards show (the show's title translates as 'Battle of the Bands'), since 2007 it had been more of a celebratory festival featuring the best K-pop acts around. The 2015 edition was no exception, with massive names such as Psy, Girls' Generation, Shinee, EXO, Apink, AOA and VIXX topping the bill, alongside JYP Entertainment heavyweights 2PM and Got7. It also featured the best up-and-coming acts, including GFriend, Red Velvet, Lovelyz, Monsta X, Seventeen, iKon and, of course, Twice.

The live extravaganza took place on 27 December 2015 and it was the newest of all the acts that kicked off the show – Twice. They had pre-recorded a video especially for the show and it was a real gem. Entitled 'A History of K-pop with Twice', it started in the 1930s, with Jihyo and Tzuyu in vintage dresses and long gloves demonstrating the swing dance. It then progressed decade by decade with different pairs, dressed in the fashions of the time and performing the relevant dance style of the era. It was fun and superbly produced with, arguably, Dahyun and Mina's seventies disco dance, Chaeyoung and Sana's nineties hip-hop, and Mina and Momo's 2010s EDM catwalk being the pick of the dances.

When it came to their *Gayo Daejun* performance, Twice stuck with 'Like Ooh Ahh' but rang the changes. The girls were dressed in a mix of red and black tartan cheerleader-style outfits with their team name Twice or the Twice logo emblazoned across their chests. They put their all into a powerful and energetic remix of the track, but unfortunately the filming let them down;

the producers had cut the bridge and dance break, while the camera operators missed the intro.

Those familiar with JYP Entertainment's strategy knew the company always tried to get as much as it could out of every release. Before the year was out it had dropped dance videos of both the *Music Bank* version of 'Like Ooh Ahh' ('Remix Ver.1'), which had less gimmicky choreography than the original and some impressive formation changes, and the cheerleader (complete with pom-pom intro), high-energy *Gayo Daejun* version ('Remix Ver.2'). What's more, as a result of the festive performances, the single began to rise up the Korean charts again, so JYP Entertainment decided to promote the song again on the various music shows. By the first week of 2016, 'Like Ooh Ahh' was at number nine on the Melon (streaming) charts – the highest position yet! It brought new opportunities, too. Jihyo and Nayeon were invited to be guest MCs on an episode of *M Countdown* and the same show gave them a chance to perform 'Candy Boy' as a second song.

One measure of how successful a debut it had been is the number of product endorsements the group had been signed up for. Before they even debuted they were promoting the school uniform brand Skoolooks (which raised some controversy, with complaints that the advertisements were too suggestive). They then promoted the cinema chain CGV, the online action game Elsword and KB Kookmin Bank's credit card, and also became official ambassadors for *Snoopy: The Peanuts Movie*, dancing alongside Charlie Brown and Snoopy in a trailer and attending the premiere on Christmas Eve.

Twice were flying high. It had been a dream three months. Their single was performing well and they were winning over more fans every day. What could possibly go wrong? Unfortunately, in the high-profile world of K-pop the answer is almost anything. Through naivety, youthful high spirits, romance and passion, or occasionally criminal behaviour, it can be all too easy for K-pop idols to cause controversy or scandal. Tzuyu, the group's youngest member and still only 16, was about to learn the hard way.

In November, Twice had appeared on a TV variety show called *My Little Television*. The members introduced themselves, with the Japanese duo holding up their national flag and Tzuyu waving a Taiwanese flag to show her nationality. It only appeared in an online section of the show and no one thought anything of it. Then, in January, a Chinese-based Taiwanese artist called Huang An pointed out on the Chinese social media platform Weibo that Tzuyu had waved the flag of independent Taiwan. This was a problem as the Chinese government does not recognise Taiwan as a separate state. Huawei, the Chinese smartphone manufacturer, immediately terminated their endorsement deal with Twice and Tzuyu's forthcoming appearance on a Chinese New Year TV show was cancelled.

Poor Tzuyu had jeopardised Twice's future in a country where they could potentially have thousands of fans. JYP Entertainment immediately defended her, citing her young age, insisting she had no political agenda and issuing an apology to China, blaming themselves for not giving their artist proper guidance. A video was then uploaded to YouTube in which a sombre Tzuyu apologised, saying, 'There is only one China ... I am proud to consider myself thoroughly Chinese.' She concluded, 'I'm terribly sorry for the harm I have caused and I feel ashamed.' For Tzuyu and Twice the matter had been dealt with, but in Taiwan many supported their young star, feeling she had been bullied into apologising by the company.

However, there was no time for Tzuyu or Twice to feel sorry for themselves as their January schedule was packed. Their place as idols was confirmed by their participation in high-profile shows – some of which didn't even involve singing or dancing. Among them were the cookery show *Top 3 Chef King* and *Same Bed, Different Dreams*, in which Dahyun and Nayeon gave advice to reconcile teens and their parents (this episode featured a mother who was worried her son was throwing away a potential baseball career because he was obsessed with Twice!).

K-pop is nothing but original in devising entertainment formats in which stars can excel or embarrass themselves. Since 2010, the Idol Star Athletics Championships (Idol Games) has been a regular and very popular event. This is a mini-Olympics which pitches idol against idol in a bid to win medals at a selection of sporting events. In January 2015, Twice took their place among the 50 top K-pop groups, competing individually for their group and for a team. Twice were placed in a team called Beat to the End with BTS, Got7 and Bestie. The early events were not a great success for the girls. Chaeyoung was just edged out of the bronze medal in the 60-metre sprint by Binnie from Oh My Girl and Tzuyu completely missed the target in archery when her arrow got caught in her hair – the video clip of the incident went viral, though, so it was a victory of some sort!

The Twice girls, however, proved they are – literally – fighters, with a team of Jeongyeon, Momo and Nayeon entering the Ssireum event. Ssireum is a traditional form of wrestling in Korea where competitors grab each other's belts and attempt to pull or push their opponents to the ground. You might think it's hardly a sport for demure girl singers, but they went at it with gusto. Twice defeated Girl's Day and then Apink to set up a battle with EXID in the final. Jeongyeon and Nayeon were both beaten and although Momo, who had failed to win a bout up until then, defeated Exid's best wrestler, Hyelin, Twice had to settle for a silver medal.

It had been a whirlwind three months for Twice. They had debuted, seen their single become a fixture in the charts, won a rookie award, rode out controversy over the Skoolooks and Taiwan flag incidents, and established themselves as true idols with charisma as well as musical talent. The history of K-pop, however, is as littered with one-hit wonders as the Western pop charts, and the question now being asked of Twice was whether they could sustain their success with their next single …

5

CHEER UP

If Tzuyu and the other members needed a lift after the Taiwan flag affair, the 2016 Golden Disc Awards (GDAs) were just that. Considered by many to be the biggest, fairest and most credible of all the awards shows, the GDAs had been an annual event since 1986. The 2016 edition was staged over two days, with the ceremony celebrating its 30th anniversary. With Twice both performing and nominated for the Rookie of the Year award, Once travelled to the Kyung Hee University, in Seoul, with high hopes.

On day one of the ceremony, Twice's biggest fan, Park Jin-young, gave the group a boost with a shout-out from the stage. Incredibly, at the age of 44, he was collecting an award for his own 2015 single 'Who's Your Mama?', but he still took a moment to mention what a hard time Twice had been having and how proud he was that they cherished and took care of each other.

Day two of the GDAs might have belonged to EXO and Shinee, who took the *daesangs* and the lion's share of the prizes, but Once were delighted with their favourites, too. Their performance of 'Like Ooh Ahh' was one of the best ever. Dressed all in black, the girls looked stylish and sexy. Their live singing was stunning, the dancing on point and, for those watching on screens, the cameras zoomed in for some superb close-ups, including catching Sana's new dark grey hair and Jihyo and Jeongyeon's darker locks.

They also performed a special dance stage for the GDA audience. They were split into three sub-units: Jihyo, Mina and Momo in sensational black girl-crush outfits; Dahyun, Nayeon and Tzuyu playing it cute with plenty of *aegyo*; and Chaeyoung, Jeongyeon and Sana in black leather and lace performing quite the sexiest dance that any of the group had done. By the time they all came together, it was absolutely beyond doubt: there wasn't a poor dancer in the group. To cap the evening, Twice claimed a Rookie of the Year award and Tzuyu was able to step forward to thank her fans for cheering her up in this difficult period, as well as her parents (who were in the audience) for their constant support.

Once waited patiently for Twice to release new songs. When that might happen was a guessing game that fuelled many forums. Some groups return with new music within months after making their debut, whereas others had been known to wait nearly a year. In the meantime, there was plenty of Twice activity. Jeongyeon and her actor sister Seungyeon starred in a reality show called *We Are Siblings*, Nayeon was a judge on the *King of Mask Singer* show, while Dahyun was a big hit in *Real Men*, a reality show in which a group of celebrities endure the hardships of an army boot camp. Many Once filled in the time by repeat-watching 'Like Ooh Ahh', and on 20 March, just five months after its release, it became the most-viewed debut music video of any K-pop group, with nearly 47 million views.

For one evening only on the *Inkigayo* music show, five of Twice – Dahyun, Jeongyeon, Jihyo, Nayeon and Tzuyu – formed a new group with four members of rival girl group GFriend. The nine girls, dubbed TwiceFriend by fans, had got together to pay tribute to Girls' Generation, who had inspired so many female idols. The new ensemble performed Girls' Generation's iconic hit 'Gee', with each of them taking the place of the band's members as they copied the original choreography. They even mimicked their seniors' style, wearing brightly coloured shorts or skinny jeans and t-shirts. Possibly the stylists had their own fun with the non-English-speaking Twice members' t-shirts. Jeongyeon's said 'I heart beer', Jihyo, who had lost so much weight since *Sixteen*, had the single word 'Carbs', while *maknae* Tzuyu's bore the inappropriate legend 'Hoes, take off your clothes'!

Through March and into April Twice spent a month as the hosts of *M Countdown*. They introduced a new segment called 'Leap through time chart', where groups covered hits from past years, by performing Son Dam-bi's 2009 hit 'Saturday Night' and Lee Hyori's 'U-Go-Girl' from 2008. The performance started with the girls in all-white dresses pulling their sensual dance moves, but after the camera cut to a mirror ball, they had time-shifted ten years, back to pastel shorts and skirts, a playful bubblegum sound and cute choreography – and it fitted Twice like a glove. Once were pleased to see the focus on different members and especially excited to see more of Chaeyoung, with her new long hair, Jeongyeon and Tzuyu.

All the members were now getting plenty of air time. A new eight-episode weekly TV series called *Twice's Elegant Private Life* began in March. This was the group's own reality series in which Twice came up with their own tasks and games. It was revealed that Park Jin-young had some concerns before the filming that the group members were too nice and the series might be dull. He needn't have worried. They were likeable, funny, down-to-earth and always up for some mischief or a challenge.

There was so much to learn about the members as viewers watched them go about their daily lives and the shows produced many memorable moments. We discovered how sneaky they could be (especially when Sana needed pigs' trotters!) when they re-enacted how they managed to order take-away while trainees. In order to avoid the CCTV at the front door, which would give them away, they tied shoelaces together to form a long string and used this to lower the money to the deliveryman and to raise the food to their first-floor apartment. And we found out how terrible they were at cooking; how Momo, despite her dance skills, was beyond terrible at yoga whereas Dahyun was a natural, and how the girls had their own mirror ball and disco lights for midnight dance parties.

Other episodes saw them talking about their ideal boyfriend and recording video messages for a future partner, while in a campfire get-together they each wrote and read a letter from another member. This was perhaps the most emotional part of the whole series, as viewers saw just how close these girls had become since their debut. However, even this had its hilarious moments as Jeongyeon read her letter from Tzuyu (with a great impression of Tzuyu's Korean accent) that cut through the other tear-jerking heartfelt messages by saying, 'Thanks for showing me good online shopping websites'!

Some Onces loved the pranks most of all. In one episode, while the rest of the girls were sleeping, Mina, Jeongyeon and Nayeon drew on their faces with make-up markers. Poor Jihyo got 'Dobby' (after her supposed lookalike, Dobby the House Elf, from Harry Potter) written across her cheeks, while Dahyun had 'Eagle' across hers. The others woke up with doodles and marks all over their faces but took it in such good spirits – perhaps because they still managed to look so cute. Another funny prank involved a secret camera that revealed the members' reactions when they found themselves alone in a lift with a kissing couple (a rare public sight in Korea). Jeongyeon looked away in disbelief, Momo banged her head against the lift wall, Sana did her best not to giggle and a blushing Chaeyoung seemed to genuinely enjoy the experience. Only sharp Dahyun wasn't fooled at all, as she instantly spotted the camera, while Nayeon, fiddling around in her bag, missed the whole thing completely.

At one point renowned Korean actor Kim Min-kyo arrived to give some of them acting lessons before they put together a parody of the massively popular TV drama of the moment *Descendants of the Sun*. Chaeyoung, Dahyun, Jeongyeon and Tzuyu each donned military uniforms and, in footage still fondly recalled by Once, acted out favourite romantic scenes from the series. Watching *Elegant Private Life*, it was easy to forget that these girls were talented performers and not just nine normal friends living and having fun together, but just occasionally there was a reminder that they were working idols, thanks to behind-the-scenes footage of a photoshoot or a rehearsal.

The final episode of *Elegant Private Life* featured Twice's first group visit to Japan, where they played only the second KCON to be staged in the country. KCON promoted many aspects of Korean culture, but the culmination was two nights of performances by top K-pop acts. After so long being the foreigners in Korea, the J-Trinity (Once's affectionate nickname for Japanese members Mina, Momo and Sana) were the centre of attention. They seemed to enjoy it, teaching the others how to greet the audience in Japanese and interacting with the fans when they were on stage. Perhaps best of all, they were able to meet up with their parents, who all attended the show.

At the convention in Chiba, some 30 kilometres from Tokyo, in front of thousands of fans (their biggest audience to date), Twice performed 'Like Ooh Ahh' and 'Do it Again'. They had made a big impact in Japan, where Korean girl groups often struggled for attention, and had received a warm welcome from the assembled fans, who were even more excited when Twice returned at the end of popular headliners 2PM's set. Twice joined their seniors on stage for the raucous crowd-pleasing hit 'Hands Up'. However, while the Japanese fans focused on the J-Trinity, back in Korea Once were loving Tzuyu's short but sweet interaction with 2PM's main man, Taecyeon.

Just before the Japan trip, JYP Entertainment had announced that a new Twice EP and single would be released at the end of April. Once were not surprised as rumours had been circulating for some time, but they were still super-excited. No sooner had Twice arrived back in South Korea than the comeback began. They had hardly been away, of course. The two promotions of 'Like Ooh Ahh', the awards shows, the variety shows and the guest MCing on music shows had kept the group on the K-pop radar. No matter. In K-pop any return is known as a 'comeback' and acts are expected to present a fresh concept – a new musical or fashion style or theme.

On 17 April 2017, the first teaser for 'Cheer Up' was uploaded. It featured two photographs of the members in a line: one where they were in casual wear at night on the lawn of a house decorated with fairy lights and flags as if for a party, and the other where they were dressed in cheerleaders' outfits in a sports stadium. Once reacted with glee, immediately noting Momo had swapped her blonde look for light brown, Sana had taken her place as the group's blonde, while Mina not only looked fantastic with her shorter, shoulder-length, caramel-toned hair, but was in the centre of the line-up.

New teasers appeared daily for the next week. The next three increased the tension, as each showed three members mysteriously thrust into a state of shock and fear. Meanwhile, individual photos of the girls in their cheerleader or in mint and white athleisure outfits ramped up excitement levels further. These new shots gave off an innocent, girly vibe with just a hint of flirting, as Sana winks, Nayeon (her black hair in plaits) bites her thumbnail and Chaeyoung points down the camera lens.

By the time Twice showcased their new seven-track EP, titled 'Page Two', back at the Yes24 Live Hall in Seoul, the single 'Cheer Up', released just hours earlier, was already at number one in the Korean charts. More than that, it was an 'all-kill', meaning it topped all the daily and real-time charts in the country – a massive achievement for a group's second ever single. During the showcase Chaeyoung told how a tearful Jeongyeon had woken them all screaming, 'We placed first! I can't believe we placed first!' and they all hugged each other. On hearing the story told on stage, poor Jeongyeon broke down in tears again.

JYP had stuck with a winning team for Twice's second single, with Black Eyed Pilseung and lyricist Sam Lewis given responsibility for 'Cheer Up'. The result was another colour pop blend of hip-hop and other modern dance genres. This mix gave the song a fragmented feel, but also a unique Twice stamp. Each of the girls had an individual vocal part and the song was again held together by a ridiculously catchy chorus, as well as an excellent break by the group's rap duo. The lyrics were interesting, too, with the girls playing hard to get but being disappointed with their love interests' reactions.

The music video dropped at the same time as the single and was just as popular. It accumulated more than a million views in the first 24 hours and after five days had passed the ten million mark. Once again, JYP Entertainment had stuck with Naïve

Productions, who came up with a novel idea. Playing on the idea of the 'concept', they showed the girls through different lenses, courtesy of an only slightly freaky camera-head boyfriend.

In the group dances, the girls are dressed as cheerleader members and perform in an outdoor stadium and a basketball arena, but these are intercut with clips of them each portraying iconic characters from famous movies and TV shows. Tzuyu, in an elegant black dress and pearls, is unmistakably Audrey Hepburn's Holly Golightly, the sophisticated socialite from *Breakfast at Tiffany's*. Nayeon wields a phone and is Sidney Prescott, played by actress Neve Campbell, the heroine of the nineties horror flick *Scream* (although some claim she looks more like Drew Barrymore as Casey Becker, the movie's first victim). Momo's gun-toting action figure seems to blend *Tomb Raider*'s Lara Croft and Alice from *Resident Evil*, while Chaeyoung plays a no-nonsense, spaghetti-western-style cowboy.

Dahyun, exquisite in traditional costume and bright scarlet lipstick, takes the title role of a sixteenth-century courtesan from the TV series *Hwang Jini*, and newly blonde Sana brings back her space buns and adds some bubblegum pink gloss to take the part of clumsy teenager-turned-champion-of-justice Sailor Moon from the popular nineties Japanese manga series of that name. Jeongyeon goes to the 1994 classic comedy drama *Chungking Express* for the impish Faye, even re-creating the scene where she breaks into the police officer's room and holds an impromptu dance party, and Mina is Itsuki Fujii from the 1995 Japanese movie *Love Letter*, a poignant film that was a massive hit in South Korea as well as Japan. Only Jihyo misses out on a change of costume, but even then her scenes mirror those of Kirsten Dunst's cheerleader captain in 2000's *Bring It On*.

The video had been out a matter of days when something strange happened. People started honing in on Sana's 'Shy, Shy,

Shy' line about 50 seconds in. It was something about the way she smiled, but more than that, how she made the line sound like 'Sha, Sha, Sha'. At first Sana was upset as she thought she was being mocked for her poor English pronunciation. However, it soon dawned on her that the attention was mostly because the way she sang the phrase was so amazingly cute. Even at the showcase, the members had immediately felt an audience reaction when Sana sang it. Now the short clip was going viral and 'Shy, Shy, Shy' hashtags were proliferating on social media.

JYP Entertainment reacted quickly. The original choreography that Twice had performed at their showcase was modified to include a new action for the line involving the fists being rolled in front of the cheeks hiding a blushing face. This had been incorporated into the dance by the time the group delivered their first music show performance on *M Countdown* on 28 April. They took to the stage in identical white crop t-shirts, short white shorts and blue Twice baseball jackets: they looked wholesome but still a little too fresh and up for fun to be cutesy. The girls really seemed to enjoy performing the single and the new 'Shy, Shy, Shy' move fitted in effortlessly, as Sana duly delivered it with obvious delight.

The choreography was full of easy-to-learn point dances and sweet gestures – some maybe too sweet. The members admitted that even they cringed when they first saw the opening flower dance where Nayeon waters the seeds – the other eight members – who proceed to blossom. It gets much better from there, though, as they do the 'Cheer Up' move at the beginning of the chorus, punching both hands in the air, then transition to the iconic 'Shy, Shy, Shy' segment. However, it is not just about the moves, as the girls' adorable expressions are an integral part of the performance.

'Shy, Shy, Shy' wasn't the first K-pop meme to go viral. The Wonder Girls' early career had received a big boost when singer Sohee's charmingly gasped 'Omona' (meaning OMG!) in their single 'Tell Me' captured hearts in Korea and beyond. By accident, JYP Entertainment had found the winning formula again as the viral meme shot Twice to stardom. Many of K-pop and K-drama's biggest stars, among them BTS's Jungkook and G-Dragon, joined in the fun and were filmed mimicking the move. The dance was performed on TV shows, in playgrounds up and down the land, and even in army barracks as South Korean soldiers adopted Twice as their favourites.

Naturally, the popularity of 'Cheer Up' went in tandem with the meme. The single went to number one in the most prestigious Gaon chart and became a 'perfect all-kill' by topping all the weekly versions of the digital charts – a feat only achieved by a handful of acts each year. With their promotions just beginning, Twice could not have dreamt of a better reception for their second single.

6

A WINNING FORMULA

Regular appearances on the weekly Korean TV music shows are essential for any rookie K-pop acts aiming to establish themselves. In a world where visuals and choreography are as highly valued as the music, they give acts an opportunity to present themselves and their talents. For many groups, like Twice, who are yet to stage their own concerts, they also provide valuable experience in performing live. Competition to take part in a show is fierce, but an attractive choreography, a potential hit and the backing of a major company all help to land an act a place. Fortunately, Twice had all three.

The icing on the cake is to win a music show trophy. Each show runs its own weekly competition and determines its winners through a variety of calculations, which can include viewers' votes, streams, physical sales, social-media mentions and music-video views. Whichever system is used, winning is a big deal – especially for a new group – as it shows that they are building a fan base and are being recognised for the hard work they are putting in. Perhaps when they have won a hundred times, as Girls' Generation had at that time, or even 30 like

Twice's JYP seniors Wonder Girls, the gloss wears off a little, but for every act that first victory is very special.

In the week after Twice performed 'Cheer Up' on their comeback stage on *M Countdown* they appeared on successive days on *Music Bank, Show! Music Core, Inkigayo* (where they were given a schoolroom set and included recorded close-ups of each of the members), *Simply K-pop* and MTV's *The Show*. They were certainly working hard to make the song a success, although the way in which the shows calculate their winners mean it is virtually impossible to be victorious in the first week of a promotion. However, after a day's break the girls were back on *M Countdown*.

It was 5 May 2016, exactly a year since the first episode of *Sixteen* was broadcast. Once (including a large proportion of fanboys) were out in force, roaring the girls on with their screams as the performance began and chanting the key lines so loudly they almost brought the roof down when they reached the 'Shy, Shy, Shy' line. Twice looked great in their pink and white athleisure. Each had their name written somewhere on their outfits, some more obvious than others, with Tzuyu's emblazoned across her chest – perhaps JYP Entertainment had picked up on the interest she attracted when they performed.

M Countdown's complicated scoring system gave a maximum of 11,000 points. On that day Twice earned 10,264. It was the highest score of the year so far and a pretty incredible achievement for a rookie group, as usually only well-established acts broke the 10,000 mark. Their score was easily enough to beat nearest rival Jung Eun Ji's 'Hopefully Sky' and secure their first victory. The final scenes proved how much this meant to the girls. As Jihyo delivered the acceptance speech, she eventually gave in to the tears, and as the show played their winning hit, the members were too overcome with emotion or busy consoling one another to perform. Once celebrated their success and were super-thrilled to see Somi from *Sixteen*, who had performed earlier on the show with IOI, was there to hug her friends and one-time fellow trainees.

It was a real boost ahead of what would be a hundred days of hard work. Twice also had their EP, *Page Two*, to promote and in addition to the music shows were attending a never-ending cycle of radio shows, appearances and fan signings. Where they were invited to perform a second song from *Page Two* on the music shows, they chose the dynamic 'Touchdown'. It was an energetic bop with a 1960s feel and the catchiest of countdowns – and Dahyun had helped devise the exhausting choreography.

Page Two set out Twice's stall as a vivacious and vibrant group. 'Tuk Tok' (sometimes referred to as 'Ready to Talk') delivers some fast-paced funky hip-hop with some wonderfully flirty lyrics; 'Woohoo' was another exciting and breathless romp with Tzuyu and Sana (again) contributing some to-die-for English lines; while the EP's final track, 'My Headphones On', surprised listeners on many levels. Having brought the tempo right down, Twice delivered a chant-heavy, synth-throbbing hymn to independence (with just a little hint of insecurity) with Jungyeon's strong vocals and Jiyho's on-point English impressing.

Some fans might have found the two other *Page Two* tracks familiar. The EP's second track was a cover of a 1998 single, 'Precious Love', which was originally sung by Park Ji-yoon and written by Park Jin-young himself. The new version kept the high tempo of the original, but introduced a synth backing that gave it a more modern dance feel. Twice's line-sharing style also added a freshness, with everyone's biases getting a look in – it even included a new rap composed by Chaeyoung and Jihyo. It had a flow and a sweetness that made many pick it as their favourite track on the EP.

For those buying the physical version of *Page Two* there was a bonus: Twice's own take on the *Sixteen* theme 'I'm Gonna Be a Star'. However, if this was meant as a special treat for Once, it wasn't particularly well received. It may have worked as a 15-second teaser and had nostalgic value, but many thought it did not compare with the group's other tracks. Ok, it had plenty of energy and was anthemic, but that was all. They mostly pitied poor Nayeon, who was tasked with endlessly repeating the title line.

With 30,000 of the pre-order edition albums selling out before release day, *Page Two* was always going to be a success. It went straight to number two on the Gaon album chart, topped iTunes charts in seven countries and, even more impressively, reached number six on the *Billboard* World Albums chart. By mid-May, JYP were able to announce they had sold over 100,000 copies of the album. This was an astonishing achievement for a rookie girl group. Usually only boy bands sell that number of albums, and in the previous year Girls' Generation were the only girl group to reach the magic 100,000.

Meanwhile, 'Cheer Up' dominated the Korean digital charts throughout May and even prompted a resurgence for 'Like Ooh Aah', which made a reappearance in the top 20. It was played constantly on the radio and sung in playgrounds. Dance classes practised the choreography and Twice continued to promote it, making three or four appearances on the music shows each week.

The day after their first music show win, Twice performed on *Music Bank* and won again. In fact, all through May (and even into June, when they had finished promoting the song) they kept on winning. They would collect five consecutive wins on *Music Bank* as well as three in a row on *Inkigayo*, and three more in succession on *M Countdown*. They usually stuck with the sporting concept, wearing an assortment of different-coloured jackets, cropped tops and short pleated skirts, often carrying the group's name, logo or even the members' names, as if they were a top sports team. On *Inkigayo* on 29 May, for their goodbye stage, they thanked Once by donning fan-designed outfits: nine subtly different pink and mint t-shirts matched with white shorts and trainers.

And it wasn't just TV. Twice were working incredibly hard to keep Once happy and to earn new fans. They regularly assembled in the dorm to talk to fans on V LIVE and attended two or more fan signing sessions a week. They also played live shows whenever the opportunity arose. The timing was ideal as May was *Daedongjae* season in Korea. Similar to freshers' weeks in Western countries, universities up and down the country host these festivals to showcase the wide range of student activities they have available. The highlight of many is a free music performance in which the students – and sometimes the public, too – are treated to sets from top artists.

For a rookie group like Twice, these *Daedongjae* presented a perfect opportunity to play to a large number of young people. During May they appeared at nine different festivals. As the act with a number one hit they were crowd favourites and received a rapturous reception wherever they went. The performance at Yonsei University in Seoul, one of the biggest and most prestigious universities in Korea, is now part of Once legend after a clip of their performance went viral. The girls cleverly wore outfits in royal blue – the university colour – to match the t-shirts of most of the huge crowd, but even they could not have imagined the reaction. As they performed 'Cheer Up', the watching girls, boys, women and men alike all joined in the fan chants and singing in an ear-splitting display. If there was a moment when Twice knew they were on to something special, this was it.

At the end of the month, Twice celebrated their 'Cheer Up' music video reaching 35 million views by releasing another one. Titled 'Twice Avengers' (although it had no obvious connection to the Marvel Avengers franchise) it featured the girls on a barren planet with a flying saucer hovering overhead, dancing to 'Cheer Up' in their movie costumes – even poor Dahyun in her full-length traditional dress complete with high heels! It was slightly bizarre but huge fun.

Alongside all their other commitments, Twice members cropped up increasingly frequently on TV. However, the programme Once were waiting to see them on was *Knowing Bros*, which, although on cable TV, had established itself as one of the most influential shows in Korea. The show mixed light interviews and gentle mockery of the guests with challenges, but the on-screen chemistry and banter between the hosts – made up of comedians, former sportsmen and K-pop idols – gave it the edge on many shows.

The concept for *Knowing Bros* is a school where the hosts act as existing students and the guests as new students. When Twice appeared, they announced themselves as transferring from 'JYP High School' and even brought their school motto, 'JYP is Watching You!', to put up in the classroom. They tried to put on a bad girl act and talk back to the hosts, but only Jiyho was really up to the task, with the others, especially Dahyun and Tzuyu, far too nervous and shy to pull it off. Jeongyeon and Nayeon did, however, manage to prank host Seo Jang-hoon, with Jeongyeon crying inconsolably after he mocked her name. She even left the set to recover – only to return and reveal she had turned the tables by fooling him.

The show's youngest host by far was Heechul, a singer with boy band Super Junior. He was renowned for his ability to imitate dances, especially girl group dances. When Twice got up to perform the 'Cheer Up' choreography, he joined them as a tenth member and proved he had mastered the steps to Momo's 'Joreujima' line (which translates as 'Don't push me, it won't take long and I'll let you call me baby'). His dance, the pair performing the move together and Momo's gun-toting delivery from the video were suddenly all over social media. Many, too, noticed the mutual attraction between Momo and Heechul, but then that kind of gossip is generated freely on K-pop forums.

In June the original 'Cheer Up' video set a new record as the fastest K-pop music video to reach over 50 million views on YouTube. It was clear evidence that Twice were not only popular in South Korea, but were reaching an international audience, something that was confirmed when they were invited to perform at KCON 2016 at the start of August. KCON had been established in California in 2012 to promote Korean culture in America. It had grown bigger every year and in 2016 it had expanded to a three-day conference and show at the massive Staples Center in Los Angeles. Evening concerts featuring the cream of K-pop artists were the highlight of the event and Twice were booked to appear on the final evening, along with other rookie acts Monsta X and Astro, Korean-American singer Eric Nam, vocal duo Davichi, Girls' Generation sub-unit TTS and headliners BTS.

It was Twice's first trip to the US and they packed all they could into their short stay. Instagram posts showed them having fun on Santa Monica pier, wandering the streets of Hollywood and even plundering a convenience store for American snacks such as Lay's potato chips, yogurt pretzels and Sour Patch Kids candy. It was liberating for them to walk about unrecognised, but there were still plenty of K-pop fans screaming for them when they walked the KCON red carpet. Inside, a considerable number paraded around in Twice merchandise and attended the group's meet and greet.

Those fans among the 6,000 watching the show in the evening made Twice feel welcome when they came on stage and the group did the rest. Wearing the t-shirts of the city basketball team, LA Lakers, the girls endeared themselves to the locals and the infectious, feelgood vibe generated by their choreography and songs energised the crowd. By the end of their set, Twice had made many new friends. Later they returned to the stage in white suits with black lapels (pre-empting the similar outfits worn by BTS). Monsta X had returned with a crowd-pleasing rendition of 'Moves Like Jagger', but Twice's fabulous version of 'Uptown Funk' had the whole of the auditorium dancing.

When BTS finished the show, all the groups returned to the stage for a final farewell. Fans would scour the footage to analyse Twice members' interactions with BTS's Jungkook or Monsta X's Hyungwon, but the truth was that amid the confetti snowball fights and friendly dance battles (and Tzuyu being thrown a Yoda plushie!), they were just really enjoying the moment. No wonder their farewell tweet to the US read: 'LA!!! Yeah!!! See U soon!!!'

Twice flew back to Seoul and to JYP Entertainment. Park Jin-young always tried to engender a sense of family at his company. He wanted his trainees and idols to be proud to be JYP artists and to help each other, and his JYP Nation concerts were part of this. Every other year, he would assemble all his acts (including himself) under one roof. As trainees, the members of Twice would have dreamed of performing alongside their seniors and now that dream had come true.

The 2016 JYP Nation concert was held at the 7,500-capacity Seoul Jamsil Gymnasium (with three shows in Tokyo to follow) and had a theme of 'Mix and Match'. From the host of talent at his disposal, Jin-young created new groups or added members to existing acts to perform songs from the JYP Entertainment catalogue. He teamed Chaeyoung and Dahyun with Wonder Girls' Hyerim and Yubin in a female rap super-team; Twice joined Got7 to sing the boy band's 'Just Right'; Got7's Junior and Mark, along with 2PM's Nichkhun, brought male vocals to Nayeon, Chaeyoung and Tzuyu's 'Like Ooh Ahh'; and perhaps most popular of all was when Tzuyu and Jeongyeon sung alongside Taecyeon and Nichkhun from 2PM on the upbeat 'Summer Together'.

They looked to be having such fun, and there was more to be had. On V LIVE JYP organised a rock-paper-scissors game between all his stars to decide who would sing on a release of the JYP Nation song 'Encore'. As a result, Jungyeon, Mina, Momo and Nayeon took their place alongside Wonder Girls Yubin, Yenny and Lim, Miss A's Min, 2PM's Nichkhun and Junho, and Got7's Mark, Yugyeom and Jackson. It was an anthemic, slightly chaotic number, where lines per person were scarce, but the Twice members' contributions stood up well against those of their seniors.

In less than a year Twice had become a group valued among their peers at JYP Entertainment. They had also recorded the stand-out K-pop hit of the year in 'Cheer Up', and a poll in the autumn of 2016 put them as the second favourite act of 13- to 59-year-olds in Korea (even more popular than Girls' Generation – called SSND in Korea – who were known as 'the nation's girl group'). A poll of 13- to 29-year-olds placed three Twice members among the top 20 favourite idols: Jeongyeon at number 16, Nayeon at number 11 and Tzuyu at number three.

Equally impressively, Twice had created a strong bond with Once. Unlike some other companies which fostered an enigmatic aura around their groups – YG's strategy for Blackpink, as one example – JYP Entertainment had opted for maximum exposure. Twice members attended many fan signings and also appeared regularly on TV, as guests or MCs on talent shows such as *God's Voice* and *King of Mask Singer* or on entertainment shows like *Comedy Big League* or *Vitamin*. They also took full advantage of V LIVE. They had now made three seasons of their own reality show, *Twice TV*, and a series of individual interviews called *Beautiful Twice*, but what Once seemed to appreciate even more were the impromptu live chats, especially those that took place 'unofficially' at night in the dorm. There was never a quiet moment with Twice!

7

ONE IN A MILLION

K-pop fans are alert to the slightest whisper of a comeback. An enigmatic comment on Twitter or an outbreak of hoodie-wearing among the members (to hide hairstyle or colour changes) is enough to kickstart a rumour. So although JYP's announcement on 23 September that they were releasing a lightstick didn't necessary mean a comeback was due, it certainly got tongues wagging.

A cross between a wand and a torch, a lightstick is a must-have accessory for a K-pop fan, with fans of each group having their own distinctive designs and official colours. When the group is on stage, the lightsticks are an instant way for fans to show support without disturbing the performance. Fans can create an ocean of colour or a changing pattern co-ordinated through a phone app.

The official Twice lightstick was named the Candy Bong ('bong' meaning stick in Korean) and it was inspired by the 'Candy Boy' song on their first EP. The Candy Bong had the appearance of an oversized lollipop. It used two colours, apricot and neon-magenta (in effect a browny-peach colour and a purple-tinged pink), which, it was announced, were Twice's official colours, with JYP explaining that the apricot represented the group's freshness while the neon-magenta signified their bright energy.

As the autumn approached, Once were desperate for a comeback. So eager were they that in September, Twice's appearance, dressed in 1980s retro-themed outfits, when they performed a short song titled 'Everyone's Doing the Nori' in an advert for KB Kookmin Bank, became a must-see. And when Chaeyoung and Tzuyu joined in on the PPAP (Pen Pineapple Apple Pen) craze, it racked up hundreds of thousands of hits on YouTube.

Compared with many other fandoms, Once really didn't have long to wait, though. On 10 October JYP Entertainment uploaded a photo of a pink rollercoaster that incorporated a schedule for their comeback – an EP called *TWICEcoaster: Lane 1*. It also featured the letters 'TT' in an apricot and magenta circle. This got international fans puzzling, but most Koreans already knew 'TT' to be their emoticon for 'crying'.

The internationals caught up quickly as the intro film was released on the same day. It showed the girls in their 'Cheer Up' outfits, excited and elated after a performance. The mood is broken as they simultaneously receive a text with bad news. A montage then depicts them all pulling a sad face and making a crying action – their thumbs are horizontal in front of their faces and their forefingers point down at right angles.

Any changes to members' hair were immediately discussed by Once. Chaeyoung had grown hers long, Nayeon had opted for a shoulder-length style and, although Jeongyeon still kept hers short, it was now blonde. Dahyun garnered most attention, though. She had departed from the coloured ends she had had since *Sixteen* and had gone for an all-over vibrant pumpkin-orange look – and it was stunning.

Twicetober, as Once had named it, was happening. The teaser photos presented a slightly more mature image to those seen previously. The group set, shot in a country setting, was sweet and cute, and showed the girls as friends, hugging, holding hands and blowing (impressive) bubblegum bubbles together. The individual shots reinforced this image with demure poses in simple two-piece lavender and white outfits, although Momo's space buns and the pink stripes in Sana's black hair were still cause for much excitement. Each of the members then starred in their own 60-second 'TT' film. Dressed in a smart but homely style (although Jeongyeon was allowed a choker!), each girl is seen facing light-hearted disappointment in a task – Mina cuts a hole in her jumper, Chaeyoung ruins the picture she is painting – which results in the TT action.

In the midst of the comeback, on 20 October 2016, came the first anniversary of Twice's debut. It didn't go unmarked. The girls posted a photo of them all wearing friendship rings they had made when they went to Korea's Jeju Island on *Twice TV* and they hosted a special V LIVE chat. They relived the adventures of an incredible year, but also spoke of the hardships – especially the lack of sleep due to their packed schedule. The highlight of the anniversary party – if you forget Tzuyu finally giving Nayeon the birthday kiss she promised her a month earlier – was the unveiling of a new song. 'One in a Million' was, of course, the Twice greeting, but it was now a song for Once as well. As the track was played, the members sang along and even provided the fan chants – except Sana, who was reduced to tears with the emotion of the occasion.

'One in a Million' is a gentle-paced, sweet and uplifting track in which all the members get to sing. The heartfelt lyrics make it a perfect fan song, as they not only tell each Once that they are perfect and beautiful, but also state how Twice are there to console their fans in difficult times, just as Once provide support for them. It was sure to become a live favourite when Twice finally played their own concerts.

Four days later, they presented their *Twicecoaster* showcase at the Blue Square cultural centre in the heart of Seoul. Performing in their lavender costumes they sang a selection of their previous songs and three tracks from the new EP. The single 'TT' was revealed as another quirky but addictive Black Eyed Pilseung song. It used a steady house-influenced beat as a base for diverting electro-pop runs that announced rather than undercut the vocals. If it lacked the heavyweight choruses of the previous singles, it more than made up for that by continually throwing out super-catchy repetitions from Nayeon's opening 'Ba-ba-ba-baby' and Sana's 'Na-na-na' line to the 'I'm like TT, just like TT' of the chorus. The easy tempo, simple melody and clear vocals play well with the rapid switching of singers to make it an irresistible singalong.

For a bubblegum pop song the lyrics also deserved some credit. Even in translation, their descriptions of unrequited love and romantic anxiety for teens and 20-somethings (eating all day and still feeling hungry, lying down and watching time rush by, being irritated by their mothers' constant nagging) are totally relatable.

'TT' was released a week before Halloween. Given the success of the cosplay in their previous music videos, it was no big surprise to see them dive into the costume box again for the new video. Two young children turn up at a haunted house, but what they encounter isn't a scary trick, it's a real treat. As they go from sumptuous room to creepy corridor they encounter each Twice member in turn. The costume concept brings glamour – Jihyo as *Frozen*'s Elsa, Mina's pirate Jack Sparrow and Tzuyu as Morticia from the Addams Family; cuteness – Momo as

Tinkerbell and Chaeyoung as Ariel, the Little Mermaid; and humour in Nayeon's devil, Jeongyeon's fabulously realistic Pinocchio and Dahyun playing for laughs as Snowball the rabbit from *The Secret Life of Pets*; all while Sana, perched on the roof, maintains her 'cute sexy' image as the leather-clad Hit-Girl from *Kick-Ass*. In between each member showing off their exquisite make-up and costume, the whole group are seen dancing to the song. As hinted at in the teaser photos, their outfits are no longer schoolgirl-influenced or figure-hugging, but an array of looser-fitting, pastel blue and white short dresses and skirt-and-top combinations.

Instead of beginning the promotion of 'TT' on a music show, Twice returned to *Weekly Idol*. There they encountered the show's famous MC Doni (Jung Hyung Don) for the first time and he made sure few of them escaped his good-natured teasing. Fans now got to see the full choreography: a series of flirty, hip-swirling moves, including the *aegyo* fist-shaking 'Ba-ba-ba-baby', the hopping, sleeping move, the 'love you so much' flying kiss and, of course, the 'TT' gesture itself. There was plenty of fun, too, and fans loved the part where Jihyo pushed Nayeon into position, as if they were on *Weekly Idol*'s 'random dance' challenge, where groups have to pick up their choreography at random points.

Unlike boy bands' often energetic and complex moves, girl groups like Twice tend to devise dances that can be copied in bedrooms and dance classes with those signature point moves repeated several times during the song. Although by no means simple, with a little work it is possible to learn the 'TT' choreography, but where Twice are really skilful is the way the nine members interact. Much of the appeal of the 'TT' dance is the use of sub-groups and the constant change at the 'centre'. During the song all the members get an opportunity to be the focus of the dance, even if Chaeyoung only gets 10 seconds in total, while Dayhun gets the most time, with 50 seconds.

Twice kicked off their comeback music show promotions on 27 October by joining the *M Countdown* concert at the Korean holiday destination Jeju Island. By that time – four days after its release – 'TT' was already a massive hit. After just an hour it had brought Twice an all-kill and it stayed at number one on all Korea's live charts for five days. Meanwhile, the music video collected more than five million views on YouTube in less than 24 hours, set a new K-pop record with 10 million views in 40 hours and broke another by going on to reach 20 million views in just under five days.

Through the rest of October and into November Twice were in full promotion mode again, appearing on all the music shows. They generally performed in a selection of modest but stylish one-colour – lavender, red, black – and white autumn outfits. These included shirt dresses and a lot of knitwear, although Nayeon's denim off-the-shoulder dress from Korean design brand Lucky Chouette seemed the most popular with Once. Each performance revealed a little more about each of the members' personalities and the show audiences lapped it up. Jihyo, Mina, Dahyun and Chaeyoung had dropped a video on YouTube to demonstrate the fan chant, but from the music show performances it didn't seem as if Once needed tuition!

Twice danced their way to 12 music show victories (including five successive wins on *Music Bank*) in a little over a month's promotion. The 'TT' gesture went viral, not only in South Korea but in Japan, too, and the single spent four weeks at the top of the Gaon Digital Charts. It also went to number three on the Japan Hot 100 chart and number two on *Billboard*'s World charts. Meanwhile, the EP *TWICEcoaster: Lane 1* sold 165,000 copies in its first week, making Twice the highest-selling female K-pop act of the year.

In addition to 'TT' and 'One in a Million', the EP featured five other tracks. '1 to 10' became the most familiar to Once, as it was performed as the group's second song on the music shows. A more sedate sibling to 'TT', it had a lilting ebb and flow, a catchy chorus and as equally sweet choreography as the single. Many fans were pleased to hear Momo given more lines in the studio version, but a little disappointed to find Jihyo singing them when it came to performances – leading some Once to doubt Momo's ability to sing under the pressure of the TV cameras. It could have been a single in its own right and some Once cherish '1 to 10' as one of Twice's 'lost' hits.

Dressed in sweatshirts and jeans, Twice recorded a dance practice video for '1 to 10' and for another track, 'Jelly Jelly'. The latter is pure bubblegum: an up-tempo, feelgood bop driven by handclap riffs and sheer exuberance. Dahyun contributed to the fun, lively choreography, which is full of finger points and cheeky inserts, such as the thinking and phone-call gestures, and Chaeyoung's wink. They performed it on *Inkigayo* as their final stage at the end of promotions, and it was a real crowd-pleaser.

The other tracks on *TWICEcoaster: Lane 1* were highly rated by Once, too, and they also showed the group's versatility – none more so than the rock–guitar-based 'Ponytail', which, punctuated by the girls' shouts of 'Hey', was reminiscent of Japanese anime TV show soundtracks. K-pop had gone J-pop! Sana's 'Pinky, pinky' grabs listeners at the start of the track 'Pit-a-pat', before they're swept onwards by a foot-tapping synth rhythm and breathless vocals that relent only for the catchy 'Turn it up' chorus, while 'Next Page' illustrates how, in such a short time, their producers had learned to use the members' different voices to maximum effect. Although some of the songs have a similar feel, the vocal blend – here Chaeyoung's opening verse and Tzuyu and Mina's soft chorus stand out – creates something new. And by now Once were wondering whether the girls could make any combination of ohs, heys and yeahs sound catchy.

The success of Twice's EP and the singles had put them at the forefront of third-generation girl groups. In the autumn of 2016, their rivals were Blackpink and Red Velvet. Blackpink, a four-piece girl group developed by the YG company, had a big late-summer hit with 'Whistle', while five-girl Red Velvet, an SM company group, were also faring well with their single 'Revolver'. Blackpink had a girl-crush – sexy, chic and cool – vibe which was especially popular with listeners in the West, while Red Velvet flipped between girl crush and the more cutesy concept favoured by Korean and Asian audiences.

In their early releases, Twice appeared to share Red Velvet's dual-concept approach. However, with *TWICEcoaster: Lane 1* they shifted more towards cutesy – a girl-next-door appeal with lots of *aegyo* and sweet expressions, fewer revealing clothes and racy dances, and flat shoes! Nevertheless, the sense of fun permeating their songs and choreography, and the distinct personalities of each of the girls, ensured they could never become a stereotypical cutesy group.

As the award season approached, the online rivalry between fans intensified, especially between Once and Blackpink's fandom, known as Blinks. The group members themselves, though, were totally friendly. When they both appeared on the 6 November episode of *Inkigayo*, the girls hugged each other with glee, and it was revealed that Nayeon had been close friends with Blackpink's Jisoo and Jennie since their pre-debut days.

Whether JYP Entertainment had sensed that the public was more open to the cutesy approach or it was about differentiating Twice from their main rivals, the move seemed to work, and

Twice became more and more popular (indeed, their popularity even led to anti-fans identifying themselves as Thrice!). On 11 November, the video for 'Like Ooh-Ahh' passed 100 million views on YouTube. Twice were the first K-pop group to reach this landmark with their debut music video.

Days later, at the Melon Music Awards (MMAs), Twice received the Song of the Year award for 'Cheer Up'. Through her tears, Jihyo made their acceptance speech. This was not just any award, but the group's first *daesang*. There are many awards shows, each handing out a plethora of prizes, but a *daesang* is the name given to the three or four major prizes presented at the most prestigious ones. To win a *daesang* is to be confirmed as being in K-pop's elite, with previous winners of the MMA's Song of the Year including seminal hits such as Girls' Generation's 'Gee', Psy's 'Gangnam Style' and EXO's 'Growl'. Twice had reached that level just over a year since their debut.

There were more tears in early December at the MAMAs (Mnet Asian Music Awards) in Hong Kong. After a fine performance on the massive stage (at the time it was one of the most-watched MAMA videos ever) they were named Female Group of the Year, but, more importantly, collected their second *daesang*, with 'Cheer Up' once again named the 'Song of the Year'.

2016 had really put Twice on the K-pop map and there was still time left to treat Once to some Christmas surprises. First they dropped a special Christmas edition of *TWICEcoaster: Lane 1*. It contained the same tracks as the original release, but with a cover and photos featuring the girls in adorable Santa-style outfits. Sana again revealing her bare shoulders and Tzuyu looking super-cute in bunny ears particularly caught attention.

They performed 'TT' in the costumes for *Music Bank*, but the much-anticipated SBS *Gayo Daejeon* was the most exciting seasonal TV special. Among the festive collaborations, fans saw

Jihyo join EXO's Chanyeol, Blackpink's Rosé and indie duo 10cm for an entertaining acoustic stage which featured versions of each of their songs. Jihyo sung 'TT' as a duet with 10cm's Jungyeol, with Rosé providing some exquisite backing vocals. In the same show, Mina, Momo, Nayeon and Jeongyeon covered Sunmi's '24 Hours'. Dressed in black sparkly tops and tight shorts they put on a sensual performance which showed they were easily able to break out of that cutesy concept if they chose to. They then combined with four of GFriend in a dance cover of Wonder Girls' 'Tell Me', before all joining up with members of Got7 and Seventeen in a 'Who's Your Mama?' freak-out. Once just loved seeing their biases dancing with the boys, with Jeongyeon's moves next to Seventeen's Vernon being closely examined ...

It had been some year for the nine members of Twice. They had certainly made themselves known to the music fans of Korea and surrounding countries, where they had regularly appeared on variety and music shows. What those fans now wanted most of all was to see their idols performing live on stage: a Twice solo concert in front of hundreds, even thousands, of chanting Once ...

8

WELCOME TO TWICELAND

K-pop had long since stopped being a phenomenon limited to South Korea. Neighbouring and nearby countries had taken Korean acts to heart, but the appeal stretched all the way to North and South America, Australasia, Europe and the Middle East. BTS and EXO were leading the way for the latest generation of Korean acts and, although boy bands fared better than girl groups, Wonder Girls and Girls' Generation were still popular outside their home country.

Interest in Twice had taken off around the world with the success of 'Cheer Up' and 'TT'. Unsurprisingly, there were thousands of Once in the K-pop strongholds of the Philippines, Malaysia, Indonesia and Taiwan, but Vietnam, Thailand and Myanmar also figured in the official fan club's top ten countries. It was especially difficult for girl groups to win over fans in Japan and China, but Twice already had a loyal following in both countries. Meanwhile, outside Asia, in the USA and also in Brazil, where K-pop was incredibly popular, Once were well represented and growing in number.

What was interesting was how different areas favoured different members of the group. At home in South Korea, Nayeon and Dahyun would usually be found at the top of the polls for fan favourites, while there was little surprise that the J-Trinity – Sana, Mina and Momo – were the most popular in Japan. Tzuyu registered highly everywhere, naturally in her home country of Taiwan, but also in Thailand, Malaysia and the Philippines. In contrast, the West really took to Momo, with Chaeyoung, Jihyo and Jeongyeon also much more popular in the USA and Europe. This was just a snapshot and it could change with each comeback, but it highlighted that Twice had a diversity and were not dependent on a single or even a few key members.

Twice were eager to get out and play for their fans. As 2017 began they wasted no time in announcing that their first ever solo concerts would take place on three consecutive days, from 17 to 19 February, at the SK Olympic Handball Stadium in Seoul. What was more, there was a tantalising postscript that promised an overseas tour as well. All 10,000 tickets for the concerts sold out in just 40 minutes and excitement built.

On 14 January, the night after Twice became the first girl group since Girls' Generation in 2011 to win a *daesang* (their third) at the Golden Disc Awards, they held a V LIVE party. Playing a solo concert was an ambition that most of them had harboured since their trainee days. They discussed great concerts they had seen – Jeongyeon citing 2PM and Momo talking about a JYP show – and what they loved about them. They had seen how they could perform different versions of their songs, how much fun the artists had on stage and, most of all, they talked about the bond they had with their fans. Nayeon summed it up by saying that whenever they had played shows before, the first thing she did was find Once in the audience, but now she wouldn't have to, because they would all be Once! This feeling was why these live dates were called 'Twiceland', explained

Jihyo, because Twiceland is where Twice and Once could be together.

At *Twiceland – The Opening*, the name given to the trio of dates in Seoul, that's exactly what happened. The hall was lit like a fairyland and the concert lasted three hours and included everything Once could have wanted: their favourite Twice songs, covers, dances, costume changes, ments (time spent talking to the audience between songs) and plenty of fan service (generally being lovely to the fans by performing *aegyo*, responding to placards and banners, taking selfies with fans, etc.).

The girls took to the stage in all-white outfits with silver belts and hit the ground running with the up-tempo singalongs 'Touchdown', 'I'm Gonna Be a Star' and 'Cheer Up', before settling into some tracks from the EPs, along with 'Like Ooh Ahh'. One advantage of having a solo concert was that they could surprise their fans with something new. The middle section of the show was given over to a series of covers. Mina, Jihyo and Jeongyeon, all in white shirts and pinstripes, threw sharp move after sharp move to Madonna's 'Four Minutes'. Nayeon, Momo, Sana and Chaeyoung (sporting a new short bob) took to the floor (literally, for much of it) to Beyoncé's 'Yoncé/Partition', choreographed by Momo. And after a short but impressive piano solo by Dahyun, she was joined by Tzuyu to cover nineties Korean duo Turbo's hit 'Black Cat Nero'. This was arguably the best of the sub-unit performances and the group's young members, dressed in black cat outfits, totally rocked out, with Tzuyu showing she could deliver a mean rap when given the chance.

The mood changed again when they reunited on stage. In *Sailor Moon* costumes – pastel sailor-style tops with white flared skirts and long white socks – they performed the theme to that show and to *Cardcaptor Sakura*, another Japanese animation, as well as their own bubblegum numbers. Once were loving it as the screams and endless fan chants proved, but the show still wasn't over. Another costume change found them in red military-style tunic dresses for a series of songs ending in covers of EXO's 'Overdose' and Seventeen's recent hit 'Pretty U'. Then, taking off the red coats, they revealed their schoolgirl tartan skirt look for the final medley, which ended up bringing the house down with 'TT'.

The audience were exhausted by the emotion, the dancing and the excitement, but in order to get the group to perform an encore, fans had to complete their own missions, including showing they knew the 'TT' dance moves, guessing how many times they sang 'TT' in the song and taking a selfie with Twice members. Of course, they passed and were rewarded with the fan tribute 'One in a Million' and a repeat performance of all three of the group's hits. For those witnessing the show it was an evening they would not forget for a long, long time.

Each of the evening's farewell ments were emotional, but the final evening was especially poignant as the members explained just what the concerts meant to them. Jihyo stepped forward to tell how during her long years as a trainee she had often thought of giving up, but she was so pleased she carried on because, 'It feels like the moment I'd dreamed about is happening right now.' If that didn't tug at Once's heartstrings, Nayeon also recalled troubled times. She told how, during her time on *Sixteen*, she would hold Jeongyeon's hand and cry, or she'd find somewhere where she could just cry on her own all day. 'I will do my best so that from now,' she said, 'the only tears we shed are happy ones.'

Those outside South Korea watching the footage of *Twiceland – The Opening*, though, might have found something unusual about the audience: the number of fanboys. In fact, in South Korea it isn't odd for female groups to have male fans and Twice had built a reputation for having more fanboys than most. That isn't to say Twice didn't have a fangirl following, too, and although at Twiceland the girls might have been drowned out in the fan chants, those attending seemed to agree that a fifty–fifty split was an accurate estimate. However, it had also been confirmed that in April the group would take *Twiceland – The Opening* to Bangkok, Thailand, and Singapore, where they were assured of considerably more high–pitched chants and screams.

As euphoric as the Twice members must have felt after the Seoul concerts, there was no time for them to linger in the moment or relax. At 11.30 p.m. on the evening of the last concert they were back in the dorm appearing in a V LIVE broadcast as they counted down to the release of their new EP, *TWICEcoaster: Lane 2*. The teaser and photo album pictures were bright and fun. Across the shoots they played with two contrasting styles: a casual look with streetwear and skater or tartan skirts and a rebel schoolgirl persona with fishnets, leather and white Dr. Marten boots. This time hairstyles featured subtle colours. Jeongyeon stood out with her not–quite–so–short hair now an ash grey and tied into space buns, Nayeon had a shoulder–length style with a slight curl, Dahyun had a darker shade of red and Sana now sported a stunning pink ombre.

The photos aside, for some there actually wasn't too much to get excited about on *TWICEcoaster: Lane 2*. There were 13 tracks on the album, but most had been taken from previous releases. The CD version did include instrumental versions of all the singles and a re–mix of 'TT' by TAK, an up–and–coming K–pop producer who was gaining a strong reputation for his EDM sound. It was a more full–on, club–ready version and was appreciated by many Once (who had played the original far too much!) and even won over some new fans. However, what the album did contain were two brand–new Twice tracks: a new single, 'Knock Knock', and 'Ice Cream'.

'Knock Knock' was the first Twice single not to be composed by Black Eyed Pilseung, as JYP had opted for Collapsedone (Woo Min Lee), a songwriter highly rated by the company. He had previously worked with A-Pink, and Day6, and had been responsible for G Soul's big 2015 hit 'You'. While 'Knock Knock' possibly lacked some of the quirkiness and twists of the previous singles, it certainly had all the energy, charm and colour that fans associated with a Twice song.

Driven along by a rapid guitar and synth pulse, 'Knock Knock' has something of a retro eighties feel. With a line distribution divided as equally as could be expected in a nine-member group, the girls deliver sweet and uplifting melodies that culminate in the now-expected earworm of a chorus. The lyrics relay a simple message of how they are waiting for someone to knock on the door to their heart and, with plenty of repetition and lots of English lines for the international fans, it was a classic singalong.

Expectations were high for the accompanying music video – and it didn't disappoint. It was an *aegyo* feast with plenty of humour and a sprinkling of attitude that stopped it being over-sugared. The storyline is basic – the girls have a slumber party before venturing outside for a snowball fight only to get locked out in the cold – but it is never boring. Stop-motion techniques, speeded-up action, and edited background and costume changes inject energy and add to the fun.

Where previous videos had been gorgeous to look at, here it was the rapid succession of visual treats that demanded repeat viewing. The *aegyo* levels are sky high from the start, as members almost seem to be competing to pose with the sweetest expressions in their triple-portrait shots. Meanwhile, in the bedroom they peek out from beneath the duvet or look super-cute in their pyjamas with their hair in bunches and plaits.

The slumber party was full of choice moments. Momo played peek-a-boo, Tzuyu hugged her giant teddy bear and Chaeyoung rapped from inside a wardrobe! Scores of outfits flashed by in seconds. There was just time to catch the white outfits adorned with black graffiti, Nayeon's red jumper with a black dress, Mina wearing a baggy blue and black jumper, Dahyun's 'Dreamy-eyed idealist' t-shirt and Chaeyoung in a black-and-white-striped dress and fishnets.

There was plenty to laugh at, too: Mina getting bashed with a pillow as she begins to sing; the girls' excitement when the door-bell rings and their disappointment when they discover it's JYP in his onesie holding a keyboard (full marks for the boss's acting and sense of humour!); or Jeongyeon refusing to follow the others by performing their signature moves when they reach the bottom of the stairs, contenting herself instead with a noncha-lant wave at the camera.

The 'Knock Knock' video also indulged those K-pop fans who love a bit of intrigue. A number of groups like to spin out a narrative over several videos. BTS's ongoing story of members' lives in a parallel world and EXO's adventures as super-powered exiles from a far-off planet are two of the most obvious exam-ples. At the end of the 'TT' video, the two trick-or-treating chil-dren were shocked by the sound of hammering on the front door of the haunted house. The video then ended with some sci-fi-type synth and a 'to be continued' notice. This same synth sound was then heard at the beginning of 'Knock Knock', which then ended with the Twice members locked out and banging on the door.

Meanwhile, during the video a fairy-tale book featuring some of the characters they had played in 'TT' landed on the doormat. Distracted by the snow and the chance of a snowball fight, the girls fail to see the pages turning by themselves and the characters

– perhaps – sparking into life. Once forums discussed what it all meant. 'Knock Knock' was clearly some kind of prequel to 'TT', but the rest was the kind of conjecture that some fans loved – with some even proposing the girls had frozen to death while locked out and the Halloween characters were ghosts!

Such was the popularity of Twice that 'Knock Knock' was another perfect all-kill. It went straight to number one on the Gaon chart in South Korea, five on the *Billboard* World chart and to number 15 on Japan's Hot 100. Although sales dropped off and the single ultimately failed to match the success of 'TT', the music video was another story. Battling with BTS's 'Not Today' (in itself impressive as boy bands traditionally were more popular globally), 'Knock Knock' became the fastest K-pop video to 30 million views, reaching the total in less than six and a half days.

The choreography, illustrated by their practice video performed in full stage outfits, was full of fun formation dances. The point dances once again were easy to learn: the 'Knock Knock' dance a fast sequence that ends with the shaking of alternate fists (Jihyo explained it as like 'banging on the bathroom door'!); in the 'Peek-a-boo' you spring forward, crouching, with hands either side of your chin; and for the 'Shooting star', where the right leg is lifted twice, stretched out and planted, followed by a finger pointing to the sky and tracing the swerving descent of the falling star.

They would demonstrate these moves regularly over the next few weeks of promotion and audiences lapped them up, along with the penguin shuffle opening, the playground arm-arches, the faux knocking on one other's back and Tzuyu's wink. The girls notched up nine more wins, taking at least one victory on each of the shows, and the choreography gave the members opportunities to have fun. For instance, what would Nayeon do when she first appeared between the two lines? On their final promotion stage, she memorably signalled '500' for their 500th day since debut.

On some shows Twice were also able to perform 'Ice Cream' (sometimes known as 'Melting'), the other new song on *TWICEcoaster Lane 2*. This soft, slow ballad showed a different side to the group. A touching and simple song about having your heart melted and being in love, it allowed the girls' differing voices to come through strongly. Nayeon starred with some impressive falsetto lines, but Once were also quick to compliment Sana's soothing tones (after 'Shy, shy, shy' she had been given a few too many cute lines), Dahyun's emotional power and Chaeyoung, who proved she was more than a rapper. The song remained the under-the-radar favourite for many Onces for years to come.

From being ferried around in cars between Seoul's TV stations, Twice graduated to flying between countries. In March and April they visited Switzerland to film for *Twice TV*, Tokyo to announce their summer debut in Japan, then to Thailand and Bangkok where they re-staged *Twiceland – The Opening*. But there was one glaring difference between these and the Seoul shows – Jihyo was seated at the side of the stage for the whole performance. She had endured knee pain for over a year, but now it had become essential that she rested her leg. Even then it didn't stop Twice's leader from taking her singing role in the concerts and even joining in with the choreography while seated!

The shows, packed with 4,000 to 5,000 fans each, followed the format of the Seoul concerts with minor adjustments to the set list to include 'Knock Knock' and, in Bangkok, a Thai version of the theme to the animation series *Chibi Maruko-chan*. The welcome and reaction the group received from the fans was just as joyous and enthusiastic as back in Korea. Indeed, in both countries, Once sprang their own surprise with a fan-made video showing their love for the group. Twice was an international success – and the TWICEcoaster was flying down the track …

9

THE NATION'S FAVOURITES

While Twice were away in Thailand and Singapore, rumours of another comeback had been growing in Korea. On 1 May 2017 it was confirmed that a new EP called *Signal* was imminent. The teasers featured the girls in white and navy school-uniform-style outfits or dainty pastel pink and blue chiffon. It was a homely concept that contrasted curiously with their antennae-hands pose and the presence of an endearing blue alien.

The single released on 15 May was also titled 'Signal' and was written and produced by JYP himself. It was the first Twice song to feature the iconic 'JYP whisper'. The boss's whispering of his initials had become a trademark in songs he produced, including massive hits such as Miss A's 'Bad Girl, Good Girl', Wonder Girls' 'So Hot' and 2PM's 'Again and Again'. As JYP trainees familiar with the tradition, it meant a lot for Twice to get this sign of approval.

'Signal' had all the trappings of the songs that had made Twice so popular – the charm, the lyrical repeats, the earworm chorus and the sense of fun – but JYP had moved the sound along. He introduced a hip-hop influence driven by the booming drum and rolling bass, and instead of sweet melodies they talked and chanted the lines. He also turned the vocal format upside down. Dahyun opened the song for the first time, Tzuyu and Sana sang the chorus, Chaeyoung got to sing and, although still quite equally divided, Momo had the most lines.

The video takes the song's lyrics about being unable to get a crush to understand your feelings and applies it to the girls' attempts to get the attention of the blue alien-headed boy. Despite each of them having superpowers, they all fail: Tzuyu's gentle touch sends him spinning across the room due to her super strength, Sana's invisibility means he just walks past her and Mina's hypnotics only succeed in sending her to sleep.

Naturally the girls look fabulous, whether in the individually styled school uniforms, the yellow, blue and red block dresses with red boots or the fun retro outfits. Bright colours are everywhere, from hair slides to chunky earrings and from Jihyo's pink toy car to Jeongyeon's bright red lipstick. And if no one is quite sure why they all faint when they see the flying saucer arrive or turn into pink-headed aliens themselves in the final frame, it is still tremendous fun.

When their promotions began, fans got a better look at the stylings and dancing. The attention-grabbers were Jeongyeon, with her hair now shoulder length and blonde; Jihyo, whose dark-brown bangs emphasised those big eyes; and Nayeon's glowing red-brown colouring. The choreography was more energy sapping, but still full of memorable point dances, including the hair washing, the hand hearts, foot stomps and the signature antennae pose. Fans watching the dance practice video might have felt they could master the dance, but Momo's powerful solo version uploaded at the end of May would have made many think again.

'Signal' was an all-kill on digital charts and stayed at number one in Korea's Gaon charts for two weeks. It reached number three on the *Billboard* World charts and charted on iTunes in the UK, USA, Germany, France, Canada, Spain and Australia. Although some critics, rival fans and even some Once were critical of the song, plenty loved it. For many, 'Signal' was their introduction to Twice and it was enough to pull them into the fandom.

For Once, what they called the 'B sides' – the other tracks on the EP – often gave them a chance to hear more of their biases. *Signal* provided Chaeyoung, Mina, Sana and Jeongyeon with more opportunities to show their singing talent. The tracks were playful and upbeat with plenty of hooks and catchy choruses, in a range of styles from the soft reggae-influenced 'Three Times a Day' to the pounding beat and chants of 'Only You' (with lyrics by Wonder Girls' Ha:tfelt) and from the bubblegum pop of 'Hold Me Tight' to the soft ballad 'Someone Like Me'. The other track, 'Eyes, Eyes, Eyes', with its poppy verse and slow chorus, deserves a special mention as Jihyo wrote the lyrics for the first verse and Chaeyoung the second. And they are excellent. Like the rest of the EP they concern teenage romance, but they are cheeky and full of spirit.

'Signal' helped Twice notch up another 12 music show wins. This took their total to 45 and past F(x), Sistar and even the Wonder Girls in the list of most successful girl groups ever. They were equal with 2NE1 with only Girls' Generation ahead of them. Of course, there was no time to celebrate. On 17 and 18 June they played *Twiceland – The Opening Encore* concerts in front of 16,000 fans at the Jamsil indoor stadium in Seoul. It was a joyous occasion with a set list that incorporated 'Knock Knock', 'Signal' and 'Ice Cream'. There were new sub-unit performances with Mina and Momo gracefully dancing to Vivaldi's *Le Quattro*

Stagioni (*The Four Seasons*); Dahyun, Jeongyeon, Sana and Tzuyu covered 'Round and Round', a 1980s song by Ta-Mi that was so upbeat and fun it could have been a Twice song; while the 'sexy unit', Nayeon, Jihyo and Chaeyoung, took on Ariana Grande's 'Greedy', Chaeyoung adding a Korean rap verse to the original. Twice's young rapper had also designed the Encore t-shirt, featuring pen drawings of each of the members. They wore them as they took their final bow in front of Once, their parents and even Sana's grandmother.

The group were now focusing on an all-important trip to Japan – with only a trip to New York for another KCON as a distraction. Their show thrilled the early audience with a selection of JYP hits – they really could turn their hands to anything! – and came back to finish the evening with a medley of their own hits in front of a US audience who seemed to know the dances and the chants. Naturally they fitted in a quick shopping and tourist trip around the city with perhaps the best moment coming as Jeongyeon and Tzuyu explored Times Square. They came across a dance group covering their own 'TT' and, unrecognised, stayed and filmed the impressive street act. It was a lightning trip, but they won over new fans in a foreign country. However, in just days they faced a whole new challenge.

It was no coincidence that Twice had three Japanese members. Being successful in Japan was vital to any K-pop group with ambition – the Japanese spent more on music than any country outside the US – but despite Tokyo being just a two-hour flight from Seoul, it was a difficult challenge. Historical grievances and political tension regularly hampered relations between South Korea and Japan. Around 2010, several K-pop groups – most notably Big Bang, Girls' Generation and a girl group called Kara – had benefitted from the Korean Wave and established a big following in Japan, but it had been a tough time for many since then. However, BTS had a number one Japanese album in the autumn of 2016, proving K-pop had a future across the water.

A group with three Japanese members surely had a chance of success, especially with JYP Entertainment giving the market such high priority. A Twitter account had been up and running since February; short YouTube videos of Japanese versions of 'Like Ooh Ahh' and 'Signal' had appeared even as they promoted 'Signal' in Korea; and they spent a shorter time than usual performing on Korean music shows in order to debut in Japan.

On 20 June, Twice released a full-length Japanese version of 'TT' accompanied by a brand new video. This time there was no cosplay, just a hot summer vibe as the members pull into a drive-in movie to watch themselves perform the song in and around an empty swimming pool. The pool's colour scheme matches the girls' green and orange vests, crop tops and denim cut-down shorts, and with no storyline the video focuses on the members, their dancing, laughter and friendship. All that is missing is Jihyo in the dance scenes, as she was still suffering with her knee when the video was shot.

Twice had been making themselves known in Japan and, when they arrived in the country at the end June, they were already the subjects of a special edition of magazine *Popteen* and the cover stars of fashion mag *Vivi*. Their images were hard to miss on ads and posters in the streets and subways of Tokyo, and 'TT' was projected in pink on the iconic Tokyo Tower. It didn't need explaining – nearly every Japanese teen already knew the 'TT' pose.

The group's first Japanese album, *#Twice*, was released on 28 June 2017. It contained Japanese versions of all the singles as well as the original Korean releases. The new versions sounded strange to some Once, with the different words and phrasing (sometimes with different translations). It was difficult for Tzuyu and the

Korean girls, especially Chaeyoung and Dahyun, who had to rap in Japanese, but the J-line had been providing extra tuition and their Japanese pronunciation was deemed excellent.

On 2 July Twice performed the songs live in their sold-out *Touchdown in Japan* showcase in front of 15,000 at the Tokyo Metropolitan Gymnasium. Once in Japan joined in the fan chants and loved the cute point dances. Fans could understand what they were projecting as, just like *aegyo* in Korea, the Japanese have their own culture of cuteness, shyness and lovability, known as *kawaii*.

As well as the showcase, Twice were working hard to promote the album in Japan. They appeared on numerous breakfast and news TV shows, and on *Music Station*, the premier music show on Japanese TV. They became the first South Korean girl group to perform on the show since 2012, reflecting the impact they were making on the Japanese music scene. Many viewers were surprised that rather than letting the J-line (who had to remember to speak standard Japanese rather than their usual Kansai dialect) take the lead, the others came forward in interviews. Jihyo was particularly impressive (sharing a room with Sana must have helped), Chaeyoung seemed comfortable, and Dayhun tried really hard and didn't worry that she sometimes talked nonsense – it was funny and endearing!

On the first day of release, nearly 47,000 physical copies of *#Twice* were sold. For the next week or so it topped album charts and immediately put them among the highest-achieving K-pop acts in Japan in recent years. 'TT' reached number three in the *Billboard* Japan Hot 100 and number 17 in the Oricon charts. Talk was now of a 'third Korean Wave' spearheaded by Twice and BTS.

It was not an opportunity Twice were about to spurn. From the outside the summer of 2017 probably seemed strangely quiet for a group whose life had been a non-stop merry-go-round of recording, promoting and touring for so long, but, of course, they were still around, appearing on TV and V LIVE (now broadcasting in Japanese, too). When they did return, though, in October, it was back in Japan. This time they had a brand new song called 'One More Time', written and produced by Japanese musicians.

'One More Time' threw in what Twice did best; a lively synth and bass beat with a cheery vibe packed with sweet melodies, cute ad libs, some gentle rap, chants of 'Twice!' and an earworm chorus. The Twice sound was already in line with a lot of J-pop, which was upbeat and full of *kawaii*, so the single just amplified these elements. Considering it was so formulaic, it was a surprisingly fresh and fun bop.

The music video took a sports concept. Nayeon plays tennis against Jihyo, Chaeyoung and Dahyun face off in a boxing ring with Jeongyeon as the referee, and the others use rhythmic gymnastics equipment. This time there are no standout outfits – they spend the whole video in sportswear – and they have uniformly dark hair, except for Sana, whose locks are light brown, but the video dials up the fun with Nayeon enjoying an anime-styled super-jump to smash the ball, referee Jeongyeon joining in the boxing and the tennis match turning into a two-team ball-throwing fight. For some reason the girls then become a nine-piece rock band. It makes no sense, but for a few seconds they are the best-looking rock group in history! Meanwhile, the jumps and twists of their choreography feature a signature finger-on-the-lips move.

The nearly 100,000 people buying the single on the day of release also discovered a second Japanese track which shouldn't be overlooked by Once. 'Luv Me' is a perfect piece of bubblegum pop: simple, upbeat and blessed with a singalong chorus. A week later 'One More Time' was number one on the *Billboard* Japan Hot 100. It was the fastest-selling album (released with instrumentals of both tracks) by any South Korean girl group in Japan.

On 20 October 2017 it was the second anniversary of Twice's debut. Their recent success in Japan capped an incredible two years of hit singles, *daesang* awards, music show wins and sell-out concerts. 'The nation's girl group' was not an official title, but one bestowed on Girls' Generation to highlight the pride the country had in the group. By the summer of 2017 their reign showed signs of coming to an end. With Twice's popularity around the country – 'Cheer Up' had even been used a campaign song by both major candidates in the 2017 South Korean presidential election – they were increasingly being anointed by journalists, DJs and the public as the nation's favourites.

Twice celebrated their anniversary with a two-day fan meeting. They also filmed a special video called *Who stole Once's heart?* with each of the members playing up to their personas as they pretended to be the criminal who stole the hearts of their fans. However, the biggest treat for Once was the announcement of Twice's first full-length album, named *Twicetagram*.

If using their Instagram handle as a title wasn't a big enough clue, the teaser photos in the style of Instagram pics accompanied by the word 'Likey' firmly tied the comeback to a social media concept. There were so many photos – some shot selfie-style, some of the group partying, some featuring the girls wearing non-matching outfits in a variety of colours and styles – but what they all shared was a chic but easy vibe from Mina's frilly pink party dress and Jeongyeon's dark blue polo and red and black arm warmers to Nayeon's spaghetti-strap blue tartan dress and Chaeyoung's shiny red bandeau. The members kept the natural-looking hair colours of 'One More Time' but appeared in the prevailing Korean fashion of curtain bangs, wispily parted down the middle and perfectly framing their faces.

Twicetagram dropped on 30 October 2017, with much of the attention stolen by the simultaneous release of 'Likey', the lead single. JYP had returned to 'Cheer Up' and 'TT' producers Black Eyed Pilseung to produce the song and they struck gold again. 'Likey' was unmistakeably a Twice song; it featured all that was great about their previous hits in a three-and-a-half-minute bop. From the opening synth blast and the 'Twice' chant, it dived straight into Sana and Jihyo delivering an instantly memorable chorus capped by the glorious 'Dugeun, dugeun, dugeun' (a Korean word for the sound of a heartbeat) and a baby 'Heart, heart' chant. As the members' upbeat but sweet melodies filled the verses, the energy levels never let up, with horns, samples (including cheering children) and drum rolls driving the instrumental through to what might be Dahyun and Chaeyoung's best rap yet.

Once again, the lyrics to a Twice hit were considered by many to be fluffy and disposable, but they really resonated with many fans. On the face of it, 'Likey' is about looking pretty and getting 'likes' for photos on social media. However, the lyrics, especially the raps, speak about the pressure to look one's best and how receiving likes has become the only way to feel good about oneself. It was a sentiment with which many listeners were all too familiar.

The 'Likey' music video was something new. Jihyo takes a video camera from her school locker and films her friends' lives, but, echoing the music, the delight comes in the sheer exuberance and buoyancy of the footage. Shot in Vancouver, Canada, it is a hymn to summer in the city as Nayeon cycles, Jeongyeon rides her skateboard, Tzuyu is on rollerblades and Sana serves up ice cream. Meanwhile, the group dance on a subway train, on the waterfront, in a downtown alley and in a school locker room and hall. Of course, they look fabulous, all the time. No costumes or sportswear here, just a fashion show's worth of chic, casual summer outfits. Momo's green-and-black-striped top, Nayeon's yellow and blue dress, Mina's yellow Hide-branded vest, Tzuyu's 'Don't' blue crop-top vest and the red, white and blue dress Jeongyeon spots in a shop window and then wears in the final street dance. The list goes on and on …

A signature dance move was now taken as a given in a Twice single and 'Likey' didn't disappoint, with the L-shape finger pose accompanying the chorus. They must have known it would go viral! Amid the points, shakes, stretches, leg flicks, Dahyun dabbing again and a hundred cute poses (including a phone-screen pose), there was also a welcome return of Momo's dance break – a twisting, arm-whirling segment which she choreographed herself.

The video had ten million views on YouTube long before 24 hours had passed and set a new record for the fastest K-pop girl group video to reach 40 million views, having hit that mark in just under a week. The single went to number one on the Gaon chart in Korea and on the *Billboard* World chart, making it the best-selling K-pop song in the US, as well as number two on *Billboard*'s Japan Hot 100.

Including 'Likey', the album *Twicetagram* had 13 tracks, with *Billboard*'s K-pop expert Jeff Benjamin describing the album as 'an entire collection of incredible bubblegum hits'. He added that such was the quality of the output, 'Likey' wasn't necessarily even the strongest track. Once agreed – the single was outrageously addictive, but then *Twicetagram* was packed with great songs.

Among the most popular tracks on the album were the jazz-tinged 'Turtle', a slower number with a beautiful opening verse from Tzuyu; '24/7', with its irrepressible beat and cute raps; and the dreamy pop-rock-infused 'Missing U'. All the songs were recognisably Twice songs with that sweet and bubbly vibe, but they were differentiated by the girls' different voices and variations in style. 'FFW' was full of chants, sugar-sweet choruses and plenty of English; Nayeon's crystal vocals elevated 'Look at Me', a song penned by former Wonder Girl Hyerim; and 'Rollin'' felt very different, as if the members were off the leash and having fun with ad libs and vocal surprises. The album even concluded with a romantic lullaby, the gentle 'Sleep Tight, Good Night', which included a beautiful spoken-word segment by Sana.

Twicetagram was loved even more because all the Korean members had contributed to the songwriting. Dahyun penned the lyrics to 'Missing U', helped out by Chaeyoung on the rap parts; Nayeon and Jihyo wrote '24/7' together; Chaeyoung supplied the words for 'Don't Give Up'; and Jeongyeon came up with a fabulous evocation of infatuation for 'Love Line'. They were all emerging as true musical talents.

As Twice began their promotions (including eight more music show wins) the album matched the single by topping *Billboard*'s World Albums charts and at home it became the fastest-selling girl group album for 15 years. It reached number seven in Japan, number ten in the US iTunes chart and made the top 30 on iTunes charts in the US, UK, Canada, Spain, Brazil, France and Germany. Some of the tracks in *Twicetagram* had shown the members' growing confidence and competence in English, and to prove it in November 2017 they gave their first interview in English to *Billboard*, with Sana and Tzuyu in particular excelling. Being the nation's favourite girl group in South Korea wasn't enough for these girls. They had the rest of the world in their sights!

10

WHAT IS LOVE?

The stunning YouTube videos, and the catchy songs and dances, were at the heart of Twice's success. However, particularly in Korea, it was the personality of each of the members that helped endear the group to fans. The *Twice TV* series showing the girls' lives in the dorm, behind the scenes at music shows or on short holidays, as well as the V LIVE broadcasts where they chatted together, allowed Once to get to know their idols.

Then there were the numerous variety shows on Korean TV. Considering they were still so young, most of them were pretty shy and nearly half were not native Korean speakers, they gave a good account of themselves on the shows. Dahyun was the least shy of the group, always full of energy, ready to exchange jokes with a presenter and up for a challenge. Nayeon had a quiet confidence and could be relied upon to tease the other members, while as leader Jihyo did her duty and overcame her shyness to step forward. Jeongyeon, living up to her girl-crush image, was cool and displayed her sharp wit.

The two youngest members were quiet at first. Chaeyoung was super-cute, and although Tzuyu could get by just by looking good, she soon became loved for her hilarious deadpan responses, whether they were deliberate or accidental (such as when instead of 'JYP Nation' she mistakenly wrote 'JYP you bitch' – the words being similar in Korean). Of the Japanese trio, Sana stood out the most with her playfulness and completely infectious laugh. Momo came alive on any dancefloor challenge, but although she was cute on camera, perhaps she still lacked the confidence in her Korean to engage fully, while Mina remained quiet and elegant, and her beautiful smile captivated viewers.

Among the highlights of their 2017 appearances were their 'holiday' to Vietnam with four fortysomething comedians on *Carefree Traveller*, their appearance on *Knowing Bros*, where Momo, Dahyun and Sana danced to the same song in completely different styles; and *Weekly Idol*, which included a double-speed take on the 'Likey' choreography (even Momo's already fast dance break) and a hilarious couple of minutes when all the members queued up to plant their lips on the kiss-phobic Jeongyeon.

Probably the clip most watched by Once was from a new show called *Oppa Thinking*, where the group wrote and performed a song about themselves. It begins with them all singing the members' stage names before each steps forward (in age order, oldest to youngest) to deliver a couple of lines about their personas. Momo sings of being the dancing machine, Sana goes for 'No Sana, No Life', Jihyo belts out a 'Knock it out' line – all fun, but the real winners are Jeongyeon with her line 'once you fall for Jeongyeon, there is no way out', the 'fresh kiwi Tzuyu' and Dahyun, who steals the show with her simple 'Dubu, Dubu, Dub, Dub, Dubu – Dahyunie!' performed with adorable *aegyo*.

The girls were certainly feeling the love by Christmas 2017. They took home the Song of the Year *daesang* at the MAMA awards for 'Signal' and again were recognised as one of the top ten acts at the MMAs. 'Likey' had already amassed over 100 million views on YouTube, 'Like Ooh Aah' and 'Cheer Up' videos both had over 200 million views and 'TT' was about to hit 300 million, making them the fastest K-pop group to reach that total and the first Korean girl group to do so. And there was still time left in the year to release another single …

Although the jangly guitars and popping drumbeats provided a jolly, almost-Christmassy feel to the new track, 'Heart Shaker', it was the girls' voices that made it special – especially Nayeon's and Tzuyu's chorus. JYP had taken a back seat again as prolific K-pop producers David Amber and Sean Alexander, along with Galactika, whose previous credits included Monsta X's 'Beautiful' and AOA's 'Heart Attack', stayed safe with a dancey, feelgood song that played to the group's strengths.

The video did the same. It's set in a series of pastel-coloured, retro-styled spaces – a diner, a supermarket – connected by doors with heart-shaped windows, and the winter feeling only emerges in the final snowy scene in front of a pink railway station. The styling avoids Christmas clichés, but it does look comfy and relaxed. One set features them all in long-sleeved white tops and jeans, while in another they're wearing knitwear in a mish-mash of colours. Dark hair is still the general rule (except Jeongyeon, whose hair is now fair with a tint of orange), but enlivened by buns, bows, plaits and, in Momo's case, flowers.

The choreography is energetic with a point dance to the chorus that interweaves several moves but is not too much of a challenge. It is also full of fun spots: Tzuyu's amazing windmill hands, Jihyo's big heart, Jeongyeon recoiling at the hug part and the crazy duck walk (which Jihyo and Dahyun, who had both suffered knee injuries, must have dreaded!). It was a pretty dance, but there wasn't as much *aegyo* as in recent choreography. Some wondered if Twice were becoming more mature. If so, it was more than could be said for the international Once who misheard a Korean lyric in the song as 'Is Sana gay?' and turned it into a mass chant at live shows.

'Heart Shaker' was the lead single of a new Twice album called *Merry and Happy*. This was a Christmas re-package of *Twicetagram* with the addition of the single and another new track which gave the album its name. As a present for Once, the track 'Merry and Happy' was as festive as they come. It had sleigh bells, joyful melodies and a classic Christmas singalong chorus, and it was soon accompanied by a gorgeous video of Christmas in the Twice household complete with home-video-style inserts.

It was turning into a great Christmas for Once as Twice topped the album and single charts and appeared on music shows promoting 'Heart Shaker' throughout December. Their *Inkigayo* triumph on Boxing Day was their thirty-third, setting a K-pop record for the most wins in a calendar year. The season also saw the usual fun with a cover of Fin KL's 2000 hit 'Now', in which Dahyun shed her cuteness to join the sexy line of Momo, Mina and Nayeon, and, savoured by Once, a performance of 'Likey' where all the members switched roles. This gave Nayeon the rapper's role as Chaeyoung took Momo's dance break, Jeongyeon took over as lead vocal and Dahyun surprised many with her beautiful singing voice.

Japan hadn't been forgotten. Twice and BTS, now the leading K-pop force in Japan, took part in *Music Station*'s end-of-year pre-Christmas celebration. Then Twice were Korea's sole representatives (and the first since 2011) at *Kōhaku*, the annual Japanese New Year's Eve TV special which had been broadcast live on television and radio for over 65 years. Known (in translation) as the *Red and White Song Battle*, acts were divided into red and white teams. Twice were in the red team but performed 'TT' in sparkling silver lamé dresses with white faux-fur-lined cuffs and hems. Twice couldn't help the red team to victory, but as a group were among the favourites of the millions watching in Japan.

Just as 2018 got under way, the video to new Japanese single 'Candy Pop' was uploaded. A fluffy and bouncy three minutes of pure bubblegum from Collapsedone, the track relies heavily on Sana, Mina and Tzuyu's pre-choruses and Nayeon's chorus, which sounded as if it came straight out of a candy advert. The video was a stroke of brilliance. Anime director Naohiko Kyogoku, who made the popular *Love Live!* series (about nine girls who become idols to save their school) was enlisted to create delightful animated 2D versions of each of the Twice members. These totally cute characters transform into their real selves in order to break out of the TV set and cheer up a little girl, then are chased by the anime police through their candy-coated world.

Once loved the cute anime versions of the members and the appearance of JYP (whose uncanny likeness to *Pokémon*'s Brock was picked up by many online commenters), who comes to the girls' rescue. They were also busy searching for the 'hidden' figures that Chaeyoung had drawn in the video, which no doubt helped it reach over four million views in 24 hours, and when the song was released it went straight to the top of the charts in Japan.

It was while promoting the single on *Music Station* that Twice met Camila Cabello. The US star who had been filmed singing along to 'Candy Pop' at a fan meeting was pictured in the centre of the group doing the signature 'TT' pose. In interviews she admitted to being obsessed with 'Candy Pop', but she wasn't the only US star to notice Twice. Around the same time American singer Sabrina Carpenter included a cover version of the song in her set as she toured Japan.

Japanese Once were being spoiled as Twice appeared in their first Japanese TV commercial, promoting the phone company Y!Mobile. Dressed in smart but colourful blazers, the group took over a classroom and demonstrated their Y!Mobile dance – an adaptation of the classic 'YMCA' dance with, of course, a little of the 'TT' choreography mixed in. Meanwhile, Twice's tour, *TWICE Showcase Live Tour 2018 'Candy Pop'*, had taken them across the country as they thrilled fans in Seto, Fukuoko, Hiroshima, Osaka, Tokyo and Saitama with a set of a dozen songs.

As the tour came to a close they released a video for 'Brand New Girl', the jaunty, guitar-pop B-side of 'Candy Pop'. It saw the girls looking gorgeous in tennis whites as they played in a croquet tournament, in different-coloured dressing gowns at a slumber party and in smart outfits in which Chaeyoung stood out in her red tartan suit and Tzuyu looked stunning, her hair in an off-centre parting and pigtails tied with blue ribbon.

They looked just as good in their (mainly) black suits on the red carpet at Japan's 2018 Golden Disc Awards at the end of February, and at the ceremony it became evident just what an impact Twice had made in such a short amount of time in the country. In the Asia category they took home the New Artist of the Year, Album of the Year and Song of the Year awards, and were declared the first K-pop girl group in Japan to receive platinum certification (sales of more than 250,000 units) for a single and album in the same year.

From Japan they went to film an advert in Thailand, then on to South America. In a *Music Bank* special in Santiago, Chile, they performed several hits, with Nayeon, Momo, Mina and Chaeyoung covering Sunmi's 'Gashina' in a seductive performance that culminated in them dancing through a shower of coloured confetti. The South American fans' enthusiasm and knowledge of the chants and dances surprised even Twice themselves.

However, Once across the around the world were cheered by the promise of a new EP in April. The teaser photos were issued in March, along with the EP title and name of the lead track, *What is Love?*, and these showed fresh-faced girls with sweets and cakes against pop-art-style backgrounds and, later, posing in high-fashion streetwear. Momo was the attention-grabber here, with a short jet-black bob and bangs over her eyes, while other fun touches included Jihyo's cropped poncho-style top, Dahyun's Betty Boop Moschino t-shirt (there would be plenty more from that range in the video) and a collection of sparkling chokers and earrings.

The single 'What is Love?' was another JYP production, with help from Collapsedone. Up-tempo electro-pop, it featured the 'Twice' chant along with a series of energising staccato beats, chimes and synth chords and, of course, a snappy chorus. While Nayeon again took the lion's share of the lines and poor Mina had just one, the rest of the members all had a chance to shine in a song that describes the appeal and mystery of love for those too young to experience it – a subject many Once could relate to.

As ever, the video was all about the visuals. The storyline sees the girls watching TV together and fighting over the remote, each wanting to watch a movie depicting their idealised version of love – each starring themselves with other members taking the male roles! It cleverly allows the girls to wear cute slumber party outfits, school uniforms, stylish dance outfits for the chore-ography and fantasy costumes as they take on characters from great movie love stories.

The girls watch *The Princess Diaries* movie on TV with Nayeon as Mia, all bad perm and glasses, and Momo as geeky Lilly

Moscovitz with her backpack, hairband and over-sized spectacles. Jeongyeon and Sana re-create the classic pottery wheel scene in *Ghost* (with Jeongyeon hilariously recoiling from the kiss – again!); a statuesque Mina is Vic from French comedy *La Boum*; Sana and Tzuyu copy Uma Thurman and John Travolta's iconic dance in *Pulp Fiction*; Tzuyu herself is perfect as Claire Danes's winged Juliet (with Jeongyeon as Romeo); Jihyo goes back to school as Itsuki in Japanese drama *Love Letter*; Momo and Tzuyu take Emma Stone and Ryan Gosling's *La La Land* roles: and Dahyun and Chaeyoung pay their own laugh-out-loud homage to hitman movie *Leon*, including the classic beard and shades.

Through these scenes and the interposed dance clips, Twice parade about in some of the most beautiful clothes they have ever been seen in. Among the memorable outifts are Momo in a blue-starred Givenchy dress, Mina in a Valentino lipstick waves dress, Nayeon's banded lace mini-dress, Jeongyeon's fuschia tartan Fendi trousers and Dahyun's incredible gold and nude, pearl-encrusted halter-neck dress – all capped by the whole group in their glamourous satin ballgowns.

A few days after the video, a dance practice version was uploaded with the members dancing in comfy sweats (Mina in an oversized tartan shirt) with Jeongyeon's new pink hair immediately noticeable. It was useful for Once learning the dance, but more preferred the sequel, 'For Once ver.'. This was hilarious and showed them laughing, hugging, fighting and being totally extra in their solo parts.

The fun continued as Twice promoted 'What is Love?' on the music shows. On their comeback stage on *M Countdown* they performed in front of a set of huge sweets and cakes; on *Music Bank* they looked like nine princesses as they took to the stage in their ballgowns; and in their final stage on *Inkigayo* they wore their movie costumes – Tzuyu was in her wings, Nayeon in her dorky glasses and, although Dahyun had dispensed with the beard, she still had the shades – and Jeongyeon's hair was now a very fetching blue. They amassed an amazing 13 wins during the promotion, while the single went to number one in Korea, five in Japan and three on the *Billboard* World charts. The video broke their own record (set by 'Heart Shaker') for reaching 20, 30 and 40 million views faster than any K-pop girl group ever.

As Once had come to expect, the *What is Love?* EP also contained tracks that were well worth listening to. 'Sweet Talker', with lyrics written by the No Jam Brothers (Chaeyoung and Jeongyeon), boasted a fine chorus and an 'Ah ooh ah' line from Sana that had Once swooning. 'Ho!' with lyrics by Jihyo was a sweet bop and a triumph for the group's vocalists whose voices were distinct yet blended superbly. The rap-led 'Dejavu' offered something different – it was a quirky number that literally ground to a halt before re-starting – and the sweetly sung 'Say Yes', with its laid-back vibe, proved a great contrast to 'What is Love?' on the music shows. The real favourite, however, was 'Stuck', a track that only appeared on the CD. It's about being 'stuck' on someone and walks a tightrope between happy and sad, with the girls' singing really tugging the heartstrings.

With so many new songs since their first tour, it was time for Twice to perform in front of their fans again. Their second tour, *Twiceland Zone 2: Fantasy Park*, began on 18 May with three shows at the 6,000-capacity Jamsil Indoor Stadium in Seoul. From the moment when the nine members, dressed in white dresses, descended on ivy-covered hoop swings like angels, to the emotional goodbyes as they left the stage wearing the pink rainbow t-shirts specially designed by Chaeyoung, they had the audience in thrall.

The girls had grown in confidence, and the singing and dancing were flawless. As they changed costume – from floral outfits to pinstripe suits and from cute candy-coloured flared skirts to black lace and leather – they went through a repertoire of old and new songs. The set featured new favourites like the recent 'Sweet Talker' and 'Stuck'; different versions of older hits, including a remix of 'Signal' and an acoustic version of 'Heart Shaker'; and a crowd-pleasing cover of Winner's 2017 summer hit 'Really Really'.

As before, there was a sub-unit section where the members tried something different. In the only solo stage, a suited and fierce Dahyun turned Rain's 'Rainism' into 'Dahyunism'; while Jihyo, Momo and Tzuyu performed a full-blooded version of Beyoncé's 'End of Time'; and Sana, Chaeyoung and Mina covered 'Oppa' by Wax. Most savoured by Once was a sultry and grinding take on Baek Ji Young and 2PM's Taecyeon's 2009 hit 'My Ear's Candy' by Nayeon and Jeongyeon (or 2yeon as Once called them) – a fancam upload of the duet soon amassed two million views. Anything but cutesy, this segment showed these girls could do girl crush or sexy concepts just as well.

Circus parades and beautiful dreamy backdrops created a fantasy land scenario for the performances – the snowflake set for 'Someone Like Me' was especially magical. During costume-change breaks, videos of the girls playing a series of games, including a pre-recorded Escape the Room game where the members needed the help of Once to succeed, were screened. All these elements contributed to a show that mesmerised the audience for nearly three hours. However, for all this, what made the show really special for thousands of Once in attendance was the way the Twice members interacted in such a natural way between songs, and their affectionate and relaxed relationship with the audience. The bond between Twice and Once had never seemed so strong.

Over the summer, Twice took *Twiceland Zone 2: Fantasy Park* to Japan, Singapore, Thailand and Indonesia, selling out even bigger venues than before. Everywhere they went, they received the same reception from Once – fans who knew the lyrics (even if they didn't know what they meant!), the fan chants and the dances, and who were more than willing to return the love they received from those nine girls up on stage.

11

SUMMER NIGHTS

Early in May 2018, Twice appeared on the Japanese TV show *Music Station*, performing their most recent single 'What is Love?'. What was extraordinary was that this was not a Japanese version; they sang in Korean. It was the first time a Korean act had done this on the prestigious show and it demonstrated just how popular the group were in Japan – Twice were leading the way for K-pop girl groups in what many saw as a new Korean Wave.

The other song they performed on that show was in Japanese. Titled 'Wake Me Up', it was their new Japanese single, although it was already familiar to many as it had been used in a TV advert for Nike Air Max, which featured the girls trying Double-Dutch skipping. The track, driven by feverish snares and sparkling with synth chimes, singalong melodies and a chanting chorus, perfectly suited the energetic theme and this was echoed in the official video, with the girls largely in sporting and cheerleader outfits, dancing in front of soft-hued sets.

'Wake Me Up' (although not its popular B-side, the efflorescent 'Pink Lemonade') was added to the set list as Twice then played four sold-out nights on the Japanese leg of the *Twiceland Zone 2 – Fantasy Park* tour in massive indoor arenas. There were 18,000 fans at each of two shows at Saitama Super Arena near Tokyo, with most of them singing happy birthday to Dahyun!

Even after finishing the tour, Twice were not done with Japan. In mid-June they released their first cover single, a version of the Jackson 5 (including a young Michael Jackson) 1969 classic 'I Want You Back'. It was a digital-only release and served as the theme song for Japanese teen romcom movie *Sensei Kunshu* (known internationally as *My Teacher, My Love*). The single was accompanied by a music video presented with movie-style opening credits and featuring the members as music store assistants auditioning for a spot as television performers. The video saw the girls in retro outfits – knotted work shirts with dark turned-up jeans, coloured rugby-style crop tops in the audition and suits in the TV performance – and some cute headscarves. There is also a fun touch when it emerges that the group are playing the bespectacled audition judges, too.

'I Want You Back' was a straight cover of the original single with just enough of the Twice zest and character to make it their own. It was their first all-English single and the girls made a good job of singing in a language that most of them were still learning. Despite this, it made the top ten in Japan and was boosted when another, very charming, video was released in which the *Sensei Kunshu* cast joined the group to sing along on the retro TV stage.

Their early summer in Japan had been fruitful. While there, they also journeyed to Okinawa Island off the south-west tip of the country. The white beaches and turquoise ocean of Akabaka were the perfect setting for the video for Twice's first summer comeback, 'Dance the Night Away'. Released on 9 July, it imagines the Twice members as castaways waking up on a desert island. They build a shelter, collect coconuts (thankfully they have tall Tzuyu to pick them) and call for help. However, this is Twice, so they mainly have fun: dancing, playing volleyball, swimming and preparing a party. They really don't want to be rescued!

Splashing around in the sea under a hot sun, the cool of the shade and the balmy evenings – the video totally nails the summer vibe. And Twice are dressed for it, too, in all-white fringed or layered gowns, summer dresses and swimwear. Like tropical princesses they wear exotic blooms in their hair and exquisite dangling earrings. Chaeyoung has suitably summery orange-dyed hair, Jeongyeon is now a brunette with a mid-length cut; and Jihyo has added silver ends to her brown hair. The leader also made many Once sit up and take notice with her amazing sun-kissed tan, with many immediately proclaiming that she completely owned this era.

The video was another record-breaker (13 million views within 24 hours of release), but the dance practice videos (one on the beach and another in the dance studio) also received hundreds of thousands of views, although the choreography and stamina that was required stumped many Once. Jihyo said, 'It was never this hard. It's the hardest one of all so far.'

The track itself was a joyful summer bop, but it moved away from the simpler singles to which fans had grown accustomed to a slightly more mature sound. It had a harder EDM edge and great horn section accompaniment but it retained the essential Twice bubblegum vocals and earworm chorus ingredients. *Billboard*'s K-pop expert Jeff Benjamin identified it as reaching out to a global audience and wrote how it had 'a festival-ready, electronic breakdown that wouldn't be out of a place on a Calvin Harris or David Guetta single'. It did go straight to number two in the *Billboard* World digital chart, but was a bigger success at home in Korea where it was the group's eighth consecutive number one in the first week of release. The single then battled it out with tracks like Red Velvet's 'Power Up', Shaun's 'Way Back Home', Seventeen's 'Oh My' and GFriend's 'Sunny Summer' as the hit of the summer – and, incredibly, stayed in the top 100 for another 57 weeks.

'Dance the Night Away' was the lead single in a repackaged EP titled *Summer Nights*. This also featured all the tracks from *What is Love?* (including 'Stuck') and two other new tracks that gave it a distinctive sun-soaked vibe. The upbeat 'Chillax', with its tropical house beat, steel drums, Latin-infused rhythms and lyrics telling you to let go of your worries (with a calming 'Chill and chill and relax-lax' chorus) perfectly complemented the lead single, while 'Shot Thru the Heart' was a love song full of lilting melodies and sweet vocals with just as sweet lyrics written by Momo, Sana and Mina. The J-Trinity's contribution meant it was just the *maknae* Tzuyu who was yet to co-author a Twice song.

The success of *Summer Nights* took Twice's total album sales to over two and a half million. This made them the highest-selling girl group in the history of K-pop. But they were not too grand to attend fun events such as the Idol Games that took place in August. In between events Twice members devised an impromptu game where they performed the choreography and waited for the trackside fans to identify the song and sing along, and then joined up with JYP younger brother group Stray Kids to perform the 'Dance the Night Away' choreography. With over two million watching the fan-shot videos online, Twice might not have won any medals at the championships, but they had won a lot of friends.

The fans were not just in Korea and Japan or even Thailand, Indonesia and Singapore, where Twice had played their solo

TOP LEFT: As trainees at JYP Entertainment the future Twice members looked up to, and were inspired by, the girl group Miss A, seen here at the Gaon Chart K-Pop Awards in February 2014.

TOP RIGHT: Park Jin-Young, founder and owner of JYP Entertainment, who has overseen Twice's incredible success.

MIDDLE LEFT: Twice receive their first major award – for Best New Female Artist – at the 2015 Mnet Asian Music Awards (MAMA) in Hong Kong.

BOTTOM LEFT: Twice demonstrate their 'signal' hand gesture at the showcase for the *Signal* EP in May 2017.

Twice hit the stage to promote the *What is Love?* EP in April 2018.

Twice's leader Jihyo addresses
the audience at the *What is Love?*
showcase in April 2018.

Chaeyoung's turn to speak at the
What is Love? showcase in
April 2018.

TOP LEFT: Jihyo, Nayeon and Mina show off Twice's new 'wild' look as they perform at the *Fancy You* showcase in April 2019.

TOP RIGHT: Sana returns as a blonde for the *Fancy You* comeback.

LEFT: Momo with straight black hair and bangs for the *Fancy You* comeback.

Jeongyeon at a Givenchy beauty store opening in August 2018.

Once were delighted to see Mina returning — and taking centre stage — in the teaser photograph for *Feel Special* in September 2018.

Twice (including a tanned Jihyo) in their 'Dance the Night Away' outfits in September 2018.

TOP: Twice perform at the MBC Korean Music Wave concert in September 2018.

MIDDLE: Headliners Twice pose on the red carpet at the 2018 KCON in Los Angeles, California.

BOTTOM LEFT: Mina attending the 2018 Mnet Music Awards at the Saitama Super Arena in Japan in December 2018.

ABOVE: Twice members attend the premiere of the movie *Twiceland* in Seoul in December 2018.

LEFT: Sana (left) and Jihyo (right) help raise the Christmas spirit at the 2019 SBS *Gayo Daejeon*.

Tzuyu at the Soribada Best K-Music Awards in Seoul in August 2019.

Dahyun (left) and Nayeon (below) at the photo call for the 34th Golden Disc Awards in January 2020.

concerts. There were Once in the Middle East, where *Summer Nights* had reached number four in the iTunes chart in the UAE; in Europe, where fans were petitioning JYP to stage concerts; and in South America, where Twice's recent trip to Chile had shown the passion of that continent's K-pop followers. However, thanks to KCON 2018, some US fans were able to see the group live at LA's Staples Center. It wasn't just Korean-Americans, there was a huge mix of ages and ethnicities in the crowd as Twice, the highlight of the event, played a short set that included Tzuyu, Jihyo and Momo's performance of Beyoncé's 'End of Time'. It was a teasing excerpt from the *Twiceland* show and the impressed US Once wondered when they might see the full version.

Twice were now approaching the third anniversary of their debut. There was no doubt that they had achieved many of the ambitions that both they and JYP had for those years. They were incredibly popular in Korea and surrounding countries with successive number one singles and EPs and sell-out arena concerts, and they had a growing international fan base around the world. Everything was rosy in the Twice garden. Except, maybe there was just one small issue: the cute versus crush dilemma. While some Korean and Japanese fanboys and girls were more than content with Twice's sweet and innocent concepts, in other countries many were finding them a little too cloying. They had seen the *Twiceland* special stages on video. They knew the members could get more badass and sexy, and that could make the songs more powerful. After all, that was the norm for acts in Europe or the Americas. It had seemed appropriate when the members were young, but the *maknae* Tzuyu was now 19 years old and the oldest member, Nayeon, was 23. With each release the murmurs asking for a more mature concept seemed to be getting louder.

So when the teasers for 'BDZ', the single from a new Japanese studio album, were released in early August, there was much excitement. Posing in front of a demolished wall ('BDZ' stood for 'Bulldozer'), the members wore their best don't-give-a-damn faces – they looked badass! The costumes, too, said girl crush, with black and purple as the predominant colours and the girls in above-the-knee boots, lace-up bodices and short leather skirts. Only in one group photo where their head and shoulders appear through the broken wall did they reveal the winning smiles that fans were used to.

On 17 August 2018 the track and music video dropped. The song is not as cutesy as Twice's previous Japanese releases, but some Once couldn't hide their disappointment – some even wondered if they had been pranked by JYP. To lyrics that revealed that the title 'BDZ' referred to a bulldozer that could be used to break down the guard around a crush's heart, JYP had composed an electro-pop song which had a light beat and pleas-ant melodies but lacked a hard edge. He said he deliberately created a 'cheer song' that Twice and Once could sing together, and it was indeed easy to imagine the 'Let's go, let's go' refrain ringing around arenas.

The video was something different. The usual bright setting was missing and the video began in a dark and hate-filled world. At over six minutes long, including a voiceover introduction by Nayeon, it is wholly plot-driven and the girls have to outsmart a security force guarding the Lovelies (little creatures with heart-shaped faces and ears) to bring back happiness to the world. The heist is masterminded by Twice leader Jihyo, but as soon as they enter the compound it descends into slapstick. Dahyun and Chaeyoung clumsily climb through the window, the security guys are distracted by Twice appearing on their surveillance screen – we see the choreography's signature 'salute' and 'Let's go! Let's go!' moves – and Sana steals a cheeky look at the camera after knocking out a guard. It's all good fun and, of course, the rescued Lovelies are incredibly cute!

'BDZ' was one of the songs performed by Twice when they returned to the Saitama Super Arena to appear at the Tokyo Girls Collection in September. Since 2005, the collection had been one of Japan's largest fashion festivals and Twice were the first foreign artists ever to perform on the opening stage. Suitably attired in stylish black, white and check outfits, they brought the house down in a perfect warm-up for their forthcoming tour, which consisted of eight shows across four Japanese cities.

The tour promoted their new Japanese album, also titled *BDZ*, which quickly went to number one in Japan. It brought together the Japanese singles, 'I Want You Back' and four new tracks. Of these, the ballad 'Be as One' stood out as a heartfelt expression of the closeness of the members and how important Once were to them. It was also the soundtrack to a popular five-minute 'document video' (documentary), which showed just how far they had come – many Once admitted to being reduced to tears by the footage. However, the ebullient 'L.O.V.E', the pure bubblegum sound of 'Say It Again' and the delicate 'Wishing' all had their fans, including many outside Japan.

On 20 October 2018 the third anniversary of Twice's debut was celebrated. There was a video looking back on the laughter and the tears and a celebratory V LIVE broadcast (with much food consumed!), but the outpouring of emotion from Once was astonishing. They took this opportunity to express exactly what the group meant to them and it was clear that Twice had helped many fans through difficult periods in their lives. The joy and optimism with which the girls faced life and the way they supported each other through hard times had been a motivation and an inspiration.

In their V LIVE chat, they had fantasised about having a month off. Some said how they would just sleep the whole time and it was clear that their schedule had been pretty gruelling. However, there was no let-up. The week they returned to Korea saw the video released of them recording a sweet song called 'Stay by My Side' as a soundtrack for a Japanese drama, and they filmed episodes of *Knowing Bros* and *Idol Room*. That week ended with a belated third anniversary party with Once in Seoul. The girls and their staff all attended in scary but stunning Halloween outfits, with Nayeon as Catwoman, Jeongyeon as No-Face from *Spirited Away* and Tzuyu's Corpse Bride among the most impressive. The treats for the assembled fans included previews of Korean versions of 'Be as One' and 'BDZ', but much of the talk among the assembled Once focused on a question the group had posed.

The question 'Do you like TWICE? YES or YES' had recently appeared on a subway billboard and it initiated a new comeback for the group with a single and EP both titled 'Yes or Yes'. Once had learned their lesson and did not read too much into the two sets of teaser images that showed the girls in high-end but slightly edgy outfits: Dahyun wore an animal-print dress, Jeongyeon a cropped denim jacket, Mina a zebra-print mini skirt and Tzuyu a yellow silk dress overlaid with pink tulle.

'Yes or Yes' was co-composed by David Amber, who had also worked on 'Heart Shaker'. Originally titled 'TLC' (tender loving care), it was initially taken by another, unnamed, group, but when they didn't use it JYP went back to Amber for it. 'Yes or Yes' is a dynamic pop song with hints of Motown, reggae and hip-hop underlying Twice's signature styles as they deliver some cute chants, sweet melodies and catchy hooks. Those looking for something different pointed to Mina's spoken-English introduction and the increase of lines for her, Jeongyeon, Tzuyu and

Momo, but there was no mistaking this as another fun, foot-tapping Twice hit.

Acknowledging the Halloween season, the video has a creepy beginning as chauffeur Jeongyeon (at the wheel again after her bulldozer exploits!) drives to 'Twice Square'. Once there, we see the individual members in 'mystical' settings – fortune-telling Mina with her crystal ball, Sana on the wheel of fortune, Tzuyu with a fortune cookie – as they explain that the object of their affection has no option but to return their love.

The video is full of gorgeous close-ups of the band members, with their perfect skin, peachy eye shadow or glittered eyes set off by mesmerising coloured contacts. Cut above her shoulder, Jihyo now had shorter hair than Jeongyeon, but it is Dahyun who had Once open-mouthed as she carried off a pink and purple ombre like a princess. In the dance footage the stylish outfits from the teasers are on show, especially the tartan with Chaeyoung's pleated Miu Miu red and black skirt, Nayeon, Momo and Sana in Versace checks and Jihyo in a punky red tartan dress complete with straps.

In an interview with *Paper* magazine Jihyo said, 'We spent a lot of time and put in a lot of effort to present a different aspect to our fans. From the song concept to the lively performance, we wanted to show a new part of us.' Had Twice moved on? Some Once claimed the comeback demonstrated a more mature style and the assertive 'yes or yes' lyrics did seem to be a departure from the innocent approach of previous songs, but the track was undeniably bubbly and many of the vocals still had a child-like ring. The styling reminded many of the 'Like Ooh Ahh' concept, before JYP had decided to take the cute route, and the choreography was certainly different. 'Yes or Yes' featured strong, athletic moves, as well as the hand and arm twists that fans were used to. It was more intense and incorporated hip-hop elements and body rolls, but kept the signature moves such as the 'Yes' (aka 'Ok') signs and salutes.

New or not, the fans loved it. It immediately topped the charts in South Korea and went to number five in Japan and on the *Billboard* World Albums chart. Twice even broke their own record, recording 31.4 million views in the first day, making it the seventh most-viewed music video in 24 hours. The EP did even better, hitting the top spot in Korea and Japan.

Once liked the way the B-sides gave all the members opportunities not afforded to them on the singles. Momo was allowed to sing in her own deep voice on 'Say You Love Me'; rappers Chaeyoung and Dahyun got to sing on the sunny 'LaLaLa' and showed how well their singing had progressed on the soothing ballad 'After Moon'. The girls were also developing their skills. Jeongyeon wrote the lyrics for 'LaLaLa'; Chaeyoung wrote the words for the quirky and uplifting 'Young and Wild'; and Jihyo penned poetic lyrics for the eighties-sounding 'Sunset', a song rated by many as the best on the EP. With the addition of the Korean version of 'BDZ', the EP amounted to an impressive group of cheery and heartening songs to add to Twice's growing collection.

Twice debuted 'Yes or Yes' on the inaugural M2 X Genie Music Awards (MGMA) and took home one of the ceremony's first *daesangs* with the Best Selling Artist award. Although they missed out at the MMAs (which they couldn't go to because they were headlining a free K-pop concert on the tiny Pacific island of Guam), they did attend the MAMAs. These were spread over three countries and Twice performed at the Japanese ceremony, taking a *Greatest Showman* theme. In red ringmaster jackets they put on a scintillating 10-minute performance with such power that it belied their cute reputation. Among many viewers it confirmed that Twice ranked among the great girl groups of all time.

Twice won the *daesangs* for Song of the Year (for 'What is Love?') and Best Female Group. Jihyo's acceptance speech was tear-jerking. She spoke of how exhausted the group was physically, emotionally and mentally, and how they had been each other's comforters. She then turned to Once and said, 'I feel even saying it a hundred times won't be enough … but thank you sincerely … A lot of people tell us that they receive strength and energy from watching our stages, but our source of strength and energy is our fans.'

12

CHEERS AND TEARS

Between *Sixteen* and the additions of Momo and Tzuyu, JYP had created something phenomenal. The nine girls each brought something different to the group and their talents had blossomed over the three years since debut. Their public appearances, even when they were on their way through airports, were greeted by mobs of screaming fans and even fancams of their performances (still notable for the massive fanboy presence) sometimes received millions of views on YouTube.

They were also delightful to watch when off stage – on V LIVE, in behind-the-scenes videos and variety shows they came across as cute, entertaining and completely at ease in each other's company. They never denied that occasional conflicts arose within the group but they insisted that they were always resolved amicably. Nayeon once said that any disputes between members were over within a minute and the others agreed that it was easy to do so because they all talked so much! Their cheerfulness and lack of ego transmitted not only to teenage and twentysomething fans who felt in need of some joy in their lives, but also to millions who recognised that these girls were just like them.

'The Best Thing I Ever Did', Twice's 2018 Christmas single, was a sweet, piano-based love song celebrating a relationship, but many took it as an expression of the way the members felt about being part of the group – especially with a video in which they watched clips of themselves from the past year. That made the final 'Let us never change' line extra poignant. It was added to the *Yes or Yes* tracks (along with a Korean version of 'Be as One') for a festive repackage called *The Year of Yes*, which made number two in the Christmas-week charts.

Twice's schedule relaxed a little in the early months of 2019, but there was still plenty for Once to enjoy. JYP released Japanese digital versions of 'Likey' and 'What is Love?' (with music videos edited from the originals which meant Once could play 'spot the difference'), there was a new series of *Twice TV* and the girls attended the Seoul Music Awards, although they were beaten to the *daesang* by BTS. Dahyun, Chaeyoung and Tzuyu took a silver medal for archery at the Idol Games, and Chaeyoung and Tzuyu wore their official school uniforms for the last time as they graduated from high school.

JYP Entertainment had been busy, though. In early February it debuted a five-piece girl group called Itzy – the company's first girl group since Twice. Along with the rest of the JYP family, the Twice members celebrated the launch, with Tzuyu commenting that they finally had a 'sister act to cheer for'. The Twice girls knew the Itzy girls as JYP trainees who had come to watch them practise and Chaeryeong from the new ensemble had even been in *Sixteen* with them all for a brief period. Twice were now seniors, looked up to and admired just as they had looked up to and admired Miss A, although Chaeryeong was quick to point out the difference between the two groups, saying, 'Twice are lovely and beautiful while we show off girl-crush vibes as well as our bright and youthful energy.' It was clear

Itzy were to be a new force in K-pop, with their debut single 'Dalla Dalla' breaking records for YouTube views and music show wins.

Days later Twice were helping launch another new group. Remember the Lovelies, the cute figures they rescued in the 'BDZ' video? These small sprites turned out to be the members' guardians and were introduced in a special video. They were animated creatures, 20cm or so tall, with heart-shaped faces and ears. Each member had one in their own colour and temperament: Nayeon's was a sky-blue Lovely named Navely with a positive personality; Jongveley was green and cool; pink Movely was a hard worker; purple Savely was cute; Jively was apricot colour and exuded shyness; Mively was mint green and peaceful; white Davley had charisma; red Chaengvely was creative; and indigo Tzuvely was a perfectionist. They were even cuter than the girls themselves, had lots of nice touches, such as Nayeon's bunny tooth and Chaeyoung's beauty spot and a slightly clumsy Savely, and even had their own humour: Chaengvely and Tzuvely were the same height!

Twice hoped their Lovelies were looking after them as they flew to Japan in early March 2019. They were about to embark on perhaps their biggest challenge since debut: their first dome tour, taking in the cities of Osaka, Tokyo and Nagoya. They were making history as the first K-pop girl group to play a dome tour and may have wondered whether they could actually fill these huge venues with 40,000 or more of their fans. The tour was named *#Dreamday*, because when they were growing up they could only have dreamed of playing venues like these. This was especially true for the Japanese trio; Momo remembered how, as a child, she had been told that only top musicians were invited play at the Tokyo Dome and now here she was, in the first K-pop girl group ever to perform at that venue.

They needn't have worried. Japan was going Twice crazy. They had picked up prizes for *BDZ* and 'Candy Pop' at the Japanese Golden Disc Awards and their second Japanese compilation album, *#Twice 2*, went to the top of the country's album charts. It was the most successful female K-pop album since Kara's *Super Girl* in 2011. The tickets for *#Dreamday* sold out within 60 seconds of going on sale, so they had to add another date in Osaka.

From early morning on the concert days, seemingly endless lines of girls, women, boys and men formed at the venues. Once, with their synchronised Candy Bongs, banners (including the 'Once Love Twice' and others that were handed out by fan clubs) and fan chants were as much part of the show as the incredible sets. The screens displayed a series of constantly changing back-drops, elevated stages moved around, 'Candy Pop' anime dolls of the members danced alongside the real thing, a host of backing dancers filled the stage, flames leapt from the floor and the girls travelled along the massive set in individual mobile carts. Perhaps most popular of all was the giant pink Lovely (known in Japan as *Laburi*) who lowered the girls to the stage in a lift.

For their part, Twice put on a fabulous show. The whole two-and-a-half-hour set was largely populated with Japanese versions of their hits. They played 30 songs and although there were no longer sub-unit performances of covers, there was an extra dance break in 'Wake Me Up', an acoustic remix of 'Only You' and the fierce dance version of 'Dance the Night Away' that Once had seen on the MBC *Gayo* earlier in the year.

#Dreamday was a massive step and a great success for the group. They played to over 200,000 fans over the five concerts and even more saw the final concert on 6 April in Nagoya as it was screened live in movie theatres across Japan. Among the audience in Tokyo were the members of Itzy, who were as

impressed as anyone. 'Every moment of Twice's stage has touched us,' they tweeted. 'We have learned a lot. It was a precious time for Itzy to make up our minds that our group must also deliver wonderful stages like our senior, Twice.'

Nearly four whole months had now elapsed since the release of new material. Although pretty normal for most groups, it was virtually a hiatus for Twice. On 7 April 2019, Once were therefore relieved to read of not only a forthcoming world tour (including US dates) but an imminent EP and single. The subsequent teaser photos ranged from classy to casual and from playful to sultry. They were stunning but they didn't give any hints as to the direction of the new concept. Once could only discuss Chaeyoung's blonde locks, Tzuyu cuddling the most gorgeous shaggy dog and Dahyun's new blue-grey hair, which she inadvertently revealed – against instructions!

When the EP *Fancy You* and the single 'Fancy' dropped in mid-April, the will-they-won't-they discussions over Twice taking a girl-crush concept ended. Something about their presentation was definitely different. 'Fancy', which marked a return to Black Eyed Pilseung, the writers of 'TT' and 'Likey', set out the stall. It had the 'Twice!' chant, the change of tempo and the sweet chorus hook that fans had come to expect, but in the verses the synth gave it a club vibe, and the vocals were stronger and more assured. The changes were subtle. Those looking for a new direction from the group found plenty of clues, while there was still much to be enjoyed by those who cherished the lovable, ever-upbeat Twice.

At Twice's showcase, the members admitted that there had been a deliberate change and that they had toned down the bright, bubbly style that characterised their biggest hits. Chaeyoung went as far as saying, 'This album will make a turning point in our career. We want to show Twice's different side.'

However, Jeongyeon explained that the Twice signature energy was present in whatever concept they presented. This was not girl crush or 'sexy', they insisted – it was just another facet of the group and, to be fair, it was one that Once had already heard in several of the B-sides.

The video was possibly a bigger break than the music. Instead of the bright sets it felt darker and artistic shots took the place of cheeky fun. There is no story, just a series of dances and close-ups of the members against psychedelic, night-time cityscape and solar-system backgrounds with plenty of CGI trickery. As they sing and dance the girls look confident and in control, and only in the chorus are those familiar Twice smiles unleashed. For the choreography Twice had turned to Kiel Tutin, who had devised rival girl group Blackpink's recent iconic girl-crush dances. The dance was dynamic and powerful, and relied upon the nine members being precisely synchronised (incredibly, they said they mastered the routine in just two days!).

The look was bolder, too. Yes, there were the block red, yellow and black tops, shorts and mini-dresses with white trainers that could have come from previous videos, but there were also sleek and sexy black outfits with chokers, chains, zips and studs, and the final set of costumes was bolder than most they had worn before. Retro, imaginative and daring, these included Mina's Versace motifs dress, Tzuyu's half-and-half pink and red dress, Dahyun's shiny blue mini-dress and, most iconic of all, Chaeyoung's neon green and black dogtooth bell-bottom trousers with matching crop top.

If 'Fancy' hedged its bets on dispensing with cutesy Twice, then the EP *Fancy You* (itself a bold statement) didn't hold back. Maybe the bubblegum wasn't spat out, but it was definitely wrapped up for later. Over four more tracks they ventured into different music styles, the vocalists sung in a range which seemed more natural and the lyrics were direct. 'Stuck in My Head' is an obvious Twice song and a very good one at that. It has all the signature Twice elements, but they are combined with an attack and urgency. Some thought it was only that divergence in style, and that 'Fancy' just edged it in terms of catchiness, that prevented this bop from being the lead single.

The other tracks on *Fancy You* all had lyrical input from Twice members. Jihyo wrote 'Girls Like Us' an inspiring 'chase your dream' song based on her ten years as a trainee. With Charlie XCX as a co-composer it was more akin to a Western pop track. Momo contributed to 'Hot', a teasing romp of a song with an addictive bass line; Sana had a hand in the funky freak-out 'Turn it Up'; and Chaeyoung helped pen the light and quirky 'Strawberry' (she loves strawberries!), which might have been sugary but here has a soft, R'n' B feel.

The gamble, if there ever was one, of the change of concept was pretty well received. *Fancy* reached number three in South Korea and four in Japan while the video racked up 42 million views in its first day – the highest yet. *Fancy You* was a number one album in Japan and was only kept off the top in Korea by the all-conquering BTS. Interestingly, it was the group's most successful album in the US to date and headed up iTunes charts in over 25 countries, including Greece, Germany, Brazil, Mexico and others outside of Asia.

Twice's performances on the music shows in the 'Fancy' era were pretty special. They performed their comeback on stage on *M Countdown* in the eye-catching outfits from the video. Chaeyoung, in her unforgettable green and black suit and pink, centre-parted bob was the initial focus, but fans marvelled at how great all the members' styling was. Jeongyeon wore her hair long for the first time since debut, Dahyun showed off her blue-denim locks – legitimately this time – and Mina looked sensational with a high ponytail and bangs, while Sana, with long blonde hair and wearing that figure-hugging Chanel two-piece, had the dance moves that left viewers open-mouthed.

On each show they revealed a different side: sexy in all-black, powerful in white suits, flirty in soft pink and super-smart in grey and white pinstripe. They collected four music show wins, including a perfect total score on *M Countdown*, a feat that had never been achieved by a girl group and only by EXO, Big Bang, Shinee and BTS among boy bands.

On 2 May, Twice launched the Candy Bong Z, the second version of their Candy Bong lightstick. The white handle remained, while the top had a new look with a dark centre featuring the Twice 'T' logo. As before, it incorporated the official apricot and neon magenta colours, but now each of the member's individual colours was available, too, as well as several display modes. At the live shows, the Candy Bongs could connect via Bluetooth to a central control which synchronised all the fan lights and even used seat numbers to co-ordinate areas or waves of colour.

The Candy Bong Zs soon appeared in their thousands as Twice began their *Twicelights* world tour. JYP Entertainment announced that Twice had sold over six million albums worldwide and, as over half of that total had come from Korean sales, it was appropriate that the tour began in Seoul with two dates at the gigantic KSPO Dome in the city's Olympic Park. The show was totally different to the *#Dreamday* concerts in Japan, but the scale and sets completely matched the ambitions of that dome tour.

To the delight of the 10,000 Once who packed the KSPO Dome for each sell-out performance, *Twicelights* showcased each facet of the group. The concert was divided into six sections with each having its own colour reflected in the girls' outfits and special re-mixed versions of their songs to fit the mood. They opened the show in girl-crush style, dressed all in black and performing powerful rock versions of 'Stuck in My Head', 'Cheer Up' and 'Touchdown'. They then donned beautiful white dresses for the ballads, which included a re-worked but cut-short 'Heart Shaker'. While the crowd continued the singing, they changed into their red outfits and returned to take up what they called a 'sexy version' of the song.

The sets were not quite as extravagant as on the *Fantasy Zone* or *#Dreamday* productions, with the group concentrating instead on performance, and *Twicelights* saw the return of the sub-unit special stages. Sana, Dahyun and Tzuyu performed a sensual dance to Beyoncé's 'Dance for You' (because it was one of Tzuyu's favourite songs), while the cool and expressive moves in Momo and Jihyo's cover of Taemin's 'Goodbye' were simply stunning. Chaeyoung had picked Nayeon, Mina and Jeongyeon to join her in covering Lady Gaga's 'Born This Way', and the LGBT+ anthem was a daring choice for a tour that was destined for countries where such matters were still controversial.

As before, Once had to succeed in their own missions – quizzes and dances – to earn an encore of a medley of Twice hits in their original versions – with the bonus of an extended dance break in 'Fancy'. And, of course, at each show, just before the final song, 'Stuck', the members delivered emotional ments (speeches addressed to the fans). On the second of the Seoul dates, Sana stepped forward to give a particularly moving ment. At the beginning of the month, she had taken to the group's Instagram site to post about a change of era in Japan as the country's head of state Akihito abdicated in favour of his son. Some Koreans took exception to her choice of words and criticised what they saw as a lack of sensitivity to her host country. At the concert Sana spoke about the controversy and how she worried that Once would turn away from her. Wiping away tears, she expressed how grateful she was to see that they had stood by her and how much she loved them.

As Once in Bangkok, Thailand, and Manila in the Philippines enjoyed the varied elements of *Twicelights*, the group's two sides were highlighted in a duo of singles released in Japan. The first of these was 'Happy Happy', which had been used since April in a soft-drink advert featuring Twice. With its clapping beat, upbeat melodies and the repeated chant of the title, it was a song bursting with joy and that summer feeling. The video, filmed in Hawaii, reflects this atmosphere. It overflows with colour, smiles and *kawaii*, and is the Twice of pigtails, graphic t-shirts and shorts, and having fun together.

'Breakthrough' was a sister song to 'Happy Happy', a grown-up sister who was less fun, but much more cool. It certainly had a Twice feel, with sing-song melodies and a catchy chorus, but it was subtle and the members sang in a natural low register. It wasn't driven by claps or snares, but a fractured synth instrumental and the members' harmonies. The video deliberately echoes 'Happy Happy' but is doused in purple light to give a summer-evening vibe. The group wear edgy black outfits or white power suits, hair is tied up and elegant earrings are on display – and the only smiles are fleeting and enigmatic.

If this was an exercise to assess which Twice concept was more popular, JYP Entertainment were none the wiser. Both tracks reached number two in the Japanese Oricon charts and went platinum (250,000 sales) by August. Although perhaps something could be concluded from the fact that outside Japan Once seemed to agree that 'Breakthrough' was Twice's best Japanese single yet.

In the midst of the release of these singles, Once received some deeply shocking news. JYP announced that 'Mina is currently struggling with sudden extreme anxiety and insecurity towards performing on stage' and she would not be taking part in the forthcoming *Twicelights* concerts in Singapore and the US. The hashtag GetWellSoonMina was soon trending with Once adding a green (Mina's colour) circle around their profile pictures to show their support.

Although upset and concerned for Mina, fans also recognised the positive steps taken by the company. The tragic suicide of Shinee's singer Jonghyun in December 2017 had highlighted the pressures on young K-pop stars. The phrase the 'dark side of K-pop' was often used to suggest that entertainment companies had little regard for the mental health of their artists, yet it was recognised that here JYP Entertainment had taken action to protect their star.

In Singapore, just eight members took to the *Twicelights* stage. It was clear that they missed Mina, but they did a professional job in adjusting the vocal and choreography parts to put on a pretty seamless performance. For their part Once made sure everyone knew Mina was on their minds. As 'After Moon' began, fans turned their lightsticks mint green to show their love and in their video tribute to the group, screened at the show, local fans make a particular point of including an interview with Mina. It brought the eight members to tears and all spoke emotionally in the closing ments. Chaeyoung summed it up by saying, 'We all miss Mina as much as you do. Although we have received lots of energy from Onces, being nine is what Twice is.' And, through her tears, Dahyun promised, 'We'll come back as one.'

13

FEEL SPECIAL

In 2009 BoA and Wonder Girls became the first K-pop stars to chart on the *Billboard* 200 and Hot 100. It seemed that America was opening up to Korean artists. The Wonder Girls toured with the Jonas Brothers, Girls' Generation appeared on the *Late Show with David Letterman* and other K-pop groups such as Big Bang and 2NE1 tried to break into the US pop world, but all had little success. Psy's massive 2012 hit *Gangnam Style* wasn't really K-pop, but it did show that the US public were open to non-English songs. Then came BTS. In 2018, the Bangtan Boys appeared to have kicked the door open again with their sell-out concerts, appearances on TV chat shows and top ten hits 'Fake Love' and 'Boy with Luv'.

Twice had been popular among K-pop fans in the US since their debut, with 'TT' selling over 30,000 copies and *Twicetagram* reaching number one on the *Billboard* World Albums charts. The release of *Fancy You* had reached out to a bigger audience, so in 2019 it felt like it might be the right time to take the *Twicelights* tour to the States. However, Blackpink had had a disappointing response to their tour in April, despite a top 50 hit with 'Kill This

Love'. Twice had yet to feature in the *Billboard* Hot 100, had no collaborations with Western artists and were also still missing Mina.

Was the US ready for Twice? In July 2019 the reactions of 11,000 Once at the sold-out concert at the legendary LA venue The Forum suggested they definitely were, with the fan chants sung and the Candy Bong Z lightsticks waved as enthusiastically as anywhere. US fans tried hard to keep up with the Korean lyrics, but the Twice members all did their best to speak to them in English. Of course, Mina was not forgotten with the mint-green lightstick ocean, chants of 'Mina! Mina!' and the members leaving a space where she should have been in the group photo.

Twice then took a brief diversion to Mexico City. The Palacio de los Deportes was the largest venue any K-pop girl group had played in Mexico, but Once had snapped up the tickets. They gave the group a warm reception and plenty of appreciation, and found the love reciprocated. Chaeyoung told them how she had always wanted to visit the country as it had been the home of one of her favourite artists, Frida Kahlo, while Momo marvelled at the way Mexican Once danced all the way through the songs, naming them the best dancers in the world.

Back in the USA, Twice returned to the Prudential Center in Newark, which they had previously played as part of the KCON festival, but this time all 20,000 of the audience were there to see them. The ecstatic response of Once was again almost overwhelming, but also evident here were a plethora of rainbow Pride flags and banners which were especially noticeable during the cover of Lady Gaga's 'Born This Way' – the LGBT+ community were well represented among the numerous ranks of Once.

Twice ended their US tour in Chicago. If JYP had been testing the water, they had found it pretty welcoming. Even without radio or TV promotion, the group had shown they could fill large venues and thrill the crowds with their performances. Jihyo promised they would be back and for American Once it couldn't be too soon. This leg of *Twicelights* might have concluded, but Twice had another promise to keep. The previous year's concert at Kuala Lumpur in Malaysia had been cancelled at the last minute and Twice had vowed to return. Malaysian Once had supported the group since debut and were among the group's biggest fan bases. They ensured it was an emotional evening, capped by Dahyun's words about Mina: 'She wasn't able to make it, but with the light that shone from your lightsticks, I felt like she's been here with us the whole time.'

In South Korea – and across the world – Once were digesting more news. Korean news and gossip platform *Dispatch* revealed that Jihyo had been dating former Wanna One vocalist Kang Daniel, a story that was confirmed by both singers' companies. Dating is rare among K-pop stars, mainly because their punishing schedules take up so much of their time, but also because K-pop companies believe romantic liaisons damage the public image of their stars. Some contracts ban artists from having relationships, although it's not clear whether this was the case with JYP and Twice. However, the members said that dating was not allowed in the first three years of the group, so Jihyo was therefore now free to date and, as Wanna One had disbanded in January, so was Kang Daniel. Fans do sometimes see such trysts, especially those made in secret, as a betrayal, but most Once reacted positively to the news, not only sending the couple their best wishes but using social media to urge all other fans to be supportive.

The news of Jihyo dating was just one more sign of Twice's development. On 14 June 2019 Tzuyu had turned 20; the last of the members had said farewell to their teenage years. As much as many Once still loved the innocent and cutesy concepts and the bubblegum sound, it was fitting that they continued to evolve into an image and musical style that they felt comfortable with. The release of a new EP called *Feel Special* in September 2019 was part of this process; Twice were not re-inventing themselves but allowing their more mature side to emerge.

The photo and individual video teasers for *Feel Special* exuded elegance, with a sprinkling of gold throughout the concept and members wearing extravagant earrings and jewellery. These were not the main talking points for Once, though. In the week before release, two subjects dominated the conversation. First, they delighted in the fact that Mina had participated in the recordings and video. It had been her own decision to work on the EP, although she would still be sitting out the promotions and performances. Of less significance, but also hugely celebrated, was the appearance of Momo's forehead. Those words trended across the world as her video teaser revealed a bang-less Momo for the first time since Twice debuted. If this alone didn't generate excitement, there was Jeongyeon back with short hair, Sana looking like a rock chick with long cotton-candy locks and Tzuyu, to all the world a goddess in an elaborate floral head-piece, her wavy hair in shades of brown, black and grey.

The single, also called 'Feel Special', was a new kind of song for Twice in terms of lyrics. JYP had based the words of the song on personal conversations he had had with each of the members in which they shared the hardships and emotions of the four years since *Sixteen*. Mina's verse on wanting to hide from the world was particularly poignant. Despite the trials the girls had faced, though, the lyrics were anything but downbeat. They celebrated the power of friendship and love and its ability to make anyone see light at the end of their tunnel – it was a message of hope for those listeners undergoing their own tough times.

It was a serious message and one that wasn't undermined by Swedish producer Ollipop and Australian Hayley Aitken's instrumental. A straightforward dance track, it eschews gimmicks and sticks to layered synth chords and heavy bass. Chaeyoung, featuring as a vocalist, and then Tzuyu begin the song with breathless urgency, Mina's sweet and delicate verse adds poignancy, with Sana, Jihyo and Nayeon bringing the power in the chorus and Dahyun going extra hard on the rap. The bubblegum bounciness has gone, as have the chants, but in return there are real, lower-range voices and some rich harmonies. Meanwhile, if anyone doubted that this was Twice, they only had to wait for the chorus, which was is perky and catchy as ever.

The video was just as ambitious. It reflects the theme of the song and captures the members' personalities, especially their vulnerabilities. Much of the video features them alone, dressed in their own style and each trapped in a different way. Mina, in an exquisite white ballgown, wanders through a mint-green neon forest, Chaeyoung wears a futuristic metallic trouser and crop top set in an empty white-tiled dome and Tzuyu looks flawless in an extravagant floral dress, but is imprisoned in a doll's house. Their gloom only lifts when they briefly encounter their special friends – Chaeyoung comes face to face with Mina, Momo is transfixed by Tzuyu through the doll's house window, Nayeon smiles at Jihyo, and Dahyun, with her Twice-coloured umbrella (a symbol for Once), approaches the sheltering Sana. Only poor Jeongyeon remains unpaired, but she finally cheers up when she is reunited with the whole group.

What's more, the opulence of the costumes and the shimmering gold and silver that permeates the scenes is visually stunning. From Momo's black lace gown to Dahyun's embellished cowboy-style jacket and from Jihyo's double-bow mini dress to the members dancing in Marchesa Notte ballgowns, the effect is breathtaking. This is augmented by the most bling ever: hooped and dangling earrings, silver hair clips, crystal and pearl necklaces as well as shining glass skin, glossy lips and glittering eye make-up.

Further evidence of this evolution in the outlook and image of Twice could be found in the other tracks on the *Feel Special* EP. Twice members wrote lyrics for all the songs apart from the single (although they did contribute to that) and the Korean version of 'Breakthrough'. JYP Entertainment were not known as a company who let artists write their own material, but here all nine members had some input. The melting pot of musical styles – house, EDM and some hip-hop – remained the same, but the vibe was definitely more grown up. They hadn't stopped being upbeat and fun, but they were a little less sweet and playful about it.

Once again, Twice proved they were not just a singles group with a collection of B-sides that each demanded replaying. There were no fillers. Nayeon's fan-inspired 'Rainbow', with its vocal runs, high notes (including an unattributed perfect whistle-tone note) and impressive backing vocals sounded an empowering 'You can do anything' message, while Jihyo's 'Get Loud' was a warning to the haters that turned anger into a thumping, carnival-ready celebration of self-confidence.

Dahyun's 'Trick It', which she said was about telling white lies to people you love, was a perfect example of the new Twice sound. It had a fast tempo, changing beats and a real groove, but the chorus, vocals and even the 'Ah-ha ah-ha ah-ha' singalong are dialled down for a smoother, more sophisticated vibe. Many Once rated it as the EP's top track. Others favoured Momo's love–hate hymn 'Love Foolish', a booming, bass-heavy, synth-clashing, dancefloor-filler which MTV would declare the best K-pop B-side of 2019.

Then there was '21:29', a title the group couldn't agree on how to say even at the showcase. Sana settled things by asking Once in the audience, who determined it was 'Two-one-two-nine' (only in Korean). The title represented the time the members came together (after a concert in the Philippines) having all written parts for the song, which was a reply to the fan letters they had received since debut. Once's response to Mina's absence seemed to have brought the group closer to each other and the fans, and this ballad – with Dahyun and Chaeyoung both singing – was a beautiful affirmation of that.

The theme of the EP enabled the members to put into words how they made each other 'feel special'. It was an aspect of the group that fans recognised but that had never been fully expressed. Now, in an interview with *BuzzFeed*, Chaeyoung summed it up: 'Whenever we have free time we love spending it together. I can really feel the bond between all of us, because we are so aware of each other's feelings and emotions.' They had jumped at the opportunity to express themselves through their music, a change recognised by MTV who acclaimed the EP as 'proof that Twice are capable of so much more than cheery hooks'.

There was a sad irony that Mina still felt unable to perform in public with the rest of the group, though JYP Entertainment received considerable credit for handling the situation in such a sensitive manner. At the showcase performance, Twice even had to dance as a seven-member group as Jihyo sat on a chair nursing a strained neck. Fortunately, she had recovered in time for the music show performances in which the choreography, again devised by dance genius Kiel Tutin, continued their run of intense dances characterised by powerful moves, and explosive hip and arm movements. Their synchronicity even impressed rival company SM Entertainment's renowned choreographer

Mihawk Back, who shared and commented on clips from their dance practice video on Instagram.

After they performed the songs at the showcase, Nayeon told how they usually worried about chart placings and sales of their releases, but this time they were just happy that they had been able to get their message across. There was little to worry about. The single and EP went to number one on the day of release in Korea and, although it didn't stay there and was not as successful in their homeland as many of their previous hits, it hit new heights internationally. The album topped iTunes charts in 22 countries and was top ten in Brazil, France, Spain, Australia, the UK and others, as well as taking the number one spot in the iTunes worldwide album chart. Many who sat up and took notice of Twice with the release of 'Fancy' had now become dedicated Once.

The promotions lasted little over two weeks, in which time they took seven more music show wins. For Once, though, something more exciting came days after the final stage. On 4 October 2019, to celebrate their fourth anniversary with Once, the group held a special Halloween-themed fan meeting. As usual, Twice went to great efforts to dress for the occasion, with special plaudits going to Tzuyu, who looked stunning as Maleficent, Chaeyoung as Edward Scissorhands and, most hilarious of all, Dahyun as the blue genie from *Aladdin* – complete with beard and moustache. Once's focus, however, was on an un-costumed figure in their midst – Mina!

The fact that she had made such an effort to thank Once for their support wasn't lost on the fans as they cheered and cheered her return. Mina didn't dance with the group (although she joined in with some of the choreography at the side of the stage), but she did sing along to 'Fancy' and 'Feel Special'. When she stepped forward to thank Once, she immediately teared up and was hugged by the other members. By the time they had been presented with a celebration cake, Mina had left the stage, but there was no way they were going to blow the candles out without her, so Sana ran backstage to fetch her. Even if it was for a brief moment, Twice were complete again ...

14

MORE & MORE

Twice had cut short the 'Feel Special' promotions in order to prepare for their imminent trip to Japan, where they would play 11 dates in five cities in support of their new album *&Twice*. For Once, the question was would they go 'happy happy' or 'breakthrough' – ultra cutesy or the mature sound? If the single 'Fake & True', released in advance of *&Twice*, was a clue, the answer was the latter. It was pure synth-pop with a nineties house beat and some pumping brass. The message of being true to yourself fitted seamlessly alongside 'Feel Special' and the video was a gem, too. The members looked sensational in sparkling costumes and designer outfits, and everything screamed luxury. Only the lie detector, the array of illusionary objects – mirrors, VR cameras, masks, paintings – and the Adam and Eve references questioned all the opulence.

'Fake & True' featured in their sold-out (there were over a million ticket applications) *Twicelights* concerts in Japan. *&Twice* wasn't released until after the Sapporo, Chiba, Osaka and Miyagi dates, so fans at those concerts had the bonus of being the first to hear some of the songs. *&Twice* featured seven new tracks, and although they didn't all reach the quality of the *Feel Special* B-sides, those international Once who dismissed it as just a Japanese release missed out. For a start, it included 'What You Waiting For', a song that not only shows off the group's lower-range vocals, but was sung completely in English. There was also 'Stronger', another track with an empowering message about overcoming setbacks, and 'How U Doin'', a break-up song that was part-written and composed by Chaeyoung, the first time a member had been involved in creating both words and music. For those missing old-style Twice there was also the catchy 'Polish', while the album ended with another classic Twice ballad, 'The Reason Why'.

Despite Mina's appearance at the Halloween party, JYP had made it clear that fans should not expect to see her on stage in Japan. Continuing to deal with the situation with admirable sensitivity, the company insisted it was Mina's choice whether, and to what extent, she would perform, even allowing her to decide on the day of the event. Fans awaiting the first concert of the tour in Sapporo were resigned to her absence, but got an even bigger shock when they discovered that Chaeyoung would not be appearing either due to ill health.

As the Sapporo show began, Once had readied themselves to watch a seven-member group, but when Twice took to the stage there were eight. In a heartbeat, a shocked audience realised that Mina was with them. Once were ecstatic. Especially when they realised she was staying for the duration of the show. She didn't participate in the ments and games, and sat out some songs, such as 'Feel Special' and the 'Born this Way' special stage (where Nayeon, Jeongyeon and the backing dancers held hands and danced in a circle around her), but took part in the other performances, even covering Chaeyoung's parts in some songs. Things got even better just days later in Chiba. With Chaeyoung and

Mina both returning, all the members were on stage at a concert for the first time in more than four months. For the rest of the tour Once revelled in the return of OT9 (OT is a term often used in K-pop to signify 'one true' – the original).

Twice were back in Japan in December for the 2019 MAMAs. Although Mina was absent, it was her words from 'Feel Special' which, spoken in English, began Everything's All Right, the name Twice had given to their segment of the show. In terms of their evolution, this was the performance that confirmed their transformation. They delivered the R'n'B remix of 'Feel Special' with the power that audiences were used to seeing from Beyoncé or Madonna. Dressed in various sparkling gold outfits, including above-the-knee gold boots, they owned the stage, from Chaeyoung's opening through Momo and Tzuyu's mirror dance, Jihyo's power moves and Nayeon's live vocals to the exhilarating extended dance break. They then followed this up with 'Fancy', proving there was still room for fun and playfulness in their repertoire. To cap the evening, Twice took home the Best Female Group award. It was their 15th *daesang* and, fittingly, they picked it up on their 1,500th day since debut.

The Christmas fun started early with Nayeon and Dahyun joining JYP on an episode of *Knowing Bros*. As well as the Twice girls dancing alongside their mentor, the presenters had great fun teasing all three, including forcing the members to chat informally to their boss. This can be difficult for young Koreans, as they are brought up to be extremely polite to their seniors, but Dahyun in particular seemed to enjoy it! As Christmas arrived there was more excitement with an official YouTube video of Sana (wearing reindeer antlers) finally putting down her version of Ariana Grande's 'Santa Tell Me' and Tzuyu confirming her increasing confidence in a dance duet with AOA's Seolhyun.

As the New Year got under way, Once even received a surprise present at the Golden Disc Awards where, having set a record for being the first girl group to win the best album and song awards in consecutive years, Twice gave their first live performance of 'The Best Thing I Ever Did'. For some, however, the most exciting news of the season came on 2 January, when it was confirmed that Momo and Super Junior's Heechul were officially dating. Once had been following the burgeoning relationship ever since the two had met on *Knowing Bros* back in 2016. In subsequent variety shows and photos posted online, it was clear to everyone that there was a chemistry between the two and, despite the couple's 13-year age difference, Once joyfully welcomed the announcement.

There was more news for Once to digest in the following week when Jihyo posted an open letter to the fans. She was explaining a curt remark she had made on a V LIVE regarding fans' comments on her leaving the show directly after Twice's performance at the MAMAs in December. It wasn't really a serious matter in itself, but what was more worrying was the revelation that as well as Mina, she, too, had been suffering from anxiety and depression. Learning this made her MAMA performance and commitment to leading the group even more admirable. However, these mental-health issues, as well as various physical injuries, led to questions about whether Twice were overworking and had a schedule that was simply too demanding. In February, as they released a repackage of *&Twice* complete with a new (but according to Once far from their best) track 'Swing', they were due to return to Japan for four more *Twicelights* dates.

Whatever Once's fears might have been, the first of these concerts, in Fukuoka, was a cause for celebration. Not only were there nine members on stage that day, but towards the end of the show, when it came to 'Feel Special', all nine lined up for the choreography. Mina had seemed in good form throughout, but it still came as a joyful surprise. It was the first time ever they had performed the choreography on stage as a full group. Soon #ProudOfYouMina was trending at number one across the world and later a clip of the momentous event was uploaded to the official Twice Twitter account. The members had a spring in their step as they continued on to Shizuoka, but what they didn't know was that these two dates would be their last for the foreseeable future. The Covid-19 pandemic put much of the world into lockdown and arena concerts were out of the question – and that included the much-anticipated *Twicelights* in Seoul finale concerts, scheduled for early March.

Around the world, many Once were stuck at home, but Twice did their best to keep spirits up with a Twice University Fashion Club (president: Nayeon) appearing regularly on V LIVE. They always wore varsity jackets emblazoned with 'Twice' and highlights included a hilarious round of Mafia, their favourite party game, in which members have to determine who are the 'killers'; Mina trying to make a dalgona coffee (an upside-down cappuccino); and the Peach Sisters (Nayeon and Momo) doing *mukbang* (eating) videos in ASMR style. They also supported those struggling with the effects of the virus. Nayeon, Tzuyu and Dahyun all donated 50 million won ($25,000) to charity and JYP Entertainment donated 500 million won.

April 2020 saw the release of the YouTube documentary series *Seize the Light*. Through interviews with each of the members, their coaches and JYP, as well as backstage footage, the seven 20-minute episodes give a fascinating insight into the group. They talk of their childhoods, their life as trainees and how tough it is to be a member of Twice. Their schedule is unrelenting, which, combined with the pressure to do their absolute best, takes its toll on them. They all work incredibly hard to perfect the choreography and Jihyo even tells how she falls asleep at night still running through the dance moves in her head. When they explain how, on the eve of concerts they rehearse in the empty arenas through to the early hours, what really comes across is their supreme professionalism.

During the enforced break from live shows Twice also took the opportunity to open their own TikTok channel and they were soon having fun with a *Cosmopolitan* magazine challenge where each member had to re-create a short dance – after just one run-through. Their ability to remember the moves was impressive, but Chaeyoung's almost-perfect robot dance routine was unanimously declared the best. They had a few million views, but that was nothing compared to when they did a One Direction 'Still the One' dance challenge in April.

They paired up for a series of videos and the attempt by Tzuyu and Jihyo (who got two goes to even up the numbers!) was viewed over 20 million times. They followed the moves well, but it was the new hair colours that got tongues wagging: every one of them had changed their colour during lockdown. It was a blonde bonanza with Momo and Mina bleaching their black hair, Jeongyeon following with ash tones and Jihyo choosing a pretty pink-blonde. Dahyun went for royal blue, Sana now sported bright orange locks and Chaeyoung had a blue ombre. Tzuyu's change to a deep-red hue was less extreme and Nayeon appeared with a sophisticated brunette bob. Once gave their approval across the board, especially as it signalled a Twice comeback.

The concept for the *More & More* comeback was intriguing. There were three different album covers and these transitioned from dark to light. Each member had a concept film teaser in which they wore a white dress in a lush garden setting, only to change into a darker outfit after a red and black flash. Jeongyeon was the exception. She was, of course, the original girl-crush member and she went from dark to light. It all pointed to Twice embracing a darker concept.

On 1 June 2020, the seven-track EP *More & More* was released. It included a single of the same name, written by JYP, but reflecting a new deal which saw Twice music now being released by Republic Records in the US, he had collaborated with Justin Tranter, Julia Michaels, Zara Larsson and MNEK, all of whom were steeped in Western pop music. The result was a summer bop; a tropical house song with a Western-style beat-drop chorus, injected with Twice's own colourful energy. With the 'Hey!' chants and the repeated 'More, more, more' pre-chorus and sharp rap duets it even harked back to previous hits. At the same time, though, the song's lyrics, which demand more excitement and passion in a relationship that has hit its peak, demonstrate the forthright confidence characteristic of girl-crush numbers.

In the 'More & More' video, Twice find themselves in a mystical forest. In their floaty white or floral dresses they fit perfectly into the dreamy setting of exotic flowers, butterflies, rabbits and even leopards, but, just like in the teasers, a red-and-black flash brings a change. The colour is still heightened, but as the members dance in breezy bohemian maxi-dresses, there is a darker atmosphere in the forest with biblical allusions to the serpent and apple in the Garden of Eden. They break through the kaleidoscopic tunnel of light into the lakeside world where they seem to have a new freedom – existing both in the dark and light worlds. The video has a strong visual impact, but also seems to refer to Twice's own journey through the worlds of innocence and experience – until they eventually find their own place.

The 'More & More' choreography was intense and powerful and, as seen in the video, featured the welcome return of a

Momo dance break. 'Even doing the dance just once makes you feel like you've lost weight,' she remarked, and Nayeon admitted it had been a struggle to learn. The synchronisation was the most complex yet and they said this demonstrated how united they were: only nine members acting as one could pull it off successfully.

The *More & More* EP was an emphatic statement that Twice were completely at ease in their skins; they were a group that was equally comfortable singing in a high *aegyo* key or in a lower range, and they could happily flit from a distinct K-pop sound to a more Western vibe. It was a diverse and quality collection of B-sides, each of which found favour in some quarters of the fandom. The Nayeon-penned 'Make Me', in which the voices are so deep and smooth they are almost unrecognisable, and the sad but cool 'Shadow', with lyrics about hiding your true thoughts, were among the favourites. Elsewhere, Twice skipped from 'Oxygen' (originally called 'Pizza Boy' and considered as a title track in the *Feel Special* era), a playful, laid-back summer song, to the Latin-tinged 'Firework', with its bewitching chorus from Jeongyeon, and from the horn-soaked, ultimate break-up anthem 'Don't Call Me Again' to 'Sweet Summer Day', Jeongyeon and Chaeyoung's sequel to 'Dance the Night Away', a fun song that recalled the carefree Twice of earlier days.

Twice had taken another huge step. These songs not only crossed musical styles, but they confronted adult themes of self-betrayal and the darker side of romance. It had been nine months since *Feel Special*. That can be a long time in a world that moves as fast as K-pop. However, fans were stronger than ever in their response to *More & More*. It had the highest ever first-day sales for a Korean girl group and within two weeks it was the best-selling girl group EP since S.E.S.'s *A Letter from Greenland* in 2000. It went to number one in South Korea and number three in Japan, while across the world it made the *Billboard* 200 in the US and became Twice's highest entry in the UK album chart. Meanwhile, the single took just 12 days to amass a hundred million views – their fastest time yet to that total.

On 13 June, Twice, promoting 'More & More', won the first-place trophy on *Music Core*. It was their 101st music show win, taking them past Girls' Generation's record total for a girl group. Already the best-selling Korean girl group of all time, Twice had assured themselves of legendary status in the K-pop world. It had been just five years since JYP had announced the group's line-up at the finale of *Sixteen*; five years of incredible hard work and relentless schedules in which the members had overcome upsets, injuries and other setbacks, but always held on to their positivity and dedication to making Once proud.

Some of the Twice members hardly knew the others when they were first thrust together, but they now felt like family. From V LIVE broadcasts to concerts to behind-the-scenes footage it was obvious that they didn't just enjoy one another's company, but also really cared for each other. This was perhaps best illustrated by the way they had looked after Mina on her return to the stage.

They had also developed an incredible relationship with Once; a fanbase of millions in every continent of the world. The members' affection for their fans is sincere and touching and, in return, the fandom is devoted and loyal. There is a wonderful moment in the *Seize the Light* documentary in which the group are backstage in Manila, in the Philippines, listening in delight as Once rehearse their fan chants in the arena – three hours before the concert is scheduled to begin!

Many Once have been on a journey with Twice. They have watched the members grow from girls into women, seen them develop their talent and their confidence and watched their individual characters emerge. JYP, who always says he selects his idols based on their kindness and honesty, has been close to them as they have evolved as artists and knows them better than anyone. He believes that they just get better and better, insisting that, 'This is the true beginning of their story.'

And what does the future hold for Twice? In the last couple of years they have successfully developed their musical style and image to suit a twenty something group and they've done that without losing popularity. In fact, they have gained fans. The members' contributions to the writing of their songs have helped to bring a more mature outlook to their output and, given how impressive these have been, fans can surely expect to see their input increase. There is no doubt that they all have the ability to launch successful solo projects, but they have all committed themselves to a long-term future together.

The group that fans see and listen to now is very different to those nine girls who debuted in 2015, but there is a unique Twice quality that has stayed with them from 'Like Ooh Ahh' all the way through to 'More & More'. It's what fills Once with excitement before every comeback, because, whatever Twice choose to do in the future, they will remain – as they always say when they introduce themselves – 'One in a million'.

PART TWO

THE TWICE MEMBERS

15

NAYEON

Stage name: Nayeon (pronounced Na-ion)
Birth name: Im Na-yeon
Nicknames: Nabongs, Nasoong, Bunny, Squirtle,
  Fake Maknae
Lovely name: Navely
Twice colour: Sky blue
Nationality: Korean
Position: Lead vocalist, lead dancer
Date of birth: 22 September 1995
Zodiac sign: Virgo
Blood type: A
Height: 163cm (5ft 4in)

Nayeon was the first to be confirmed as a member of Twice, but it came as no great surprise. She had a superb singing voice, danced with elegance and energy, had a vivacious and confident personality, was popular with her fellow trainees and her beauty stood out even among wannabe idols. In South Korea she is, and has always been, the most popular member of the group and ranks highly among the nation's favourite idols. It seems she was born to be a star, but before debuting with Twice, even Nayeon had setbacks to overcome.

She was born in 1995 in the quiet Gangdong neighbourhood on the far eastern edge of Seoul, by the Han River, growing up with her younger sister Seoyeon and her father and mother (who sang a duet with her in a 2016 TV Christmas special). Nayeon was a cute child and when she was five entered a modelling contest. JYP Entertainment was ready to give her a contract, but her mother decided she was too young, so Nayeon returned to her schooling and proved to be a bright student.

Nayeon's desire to perform didn't diminish over the years. In 2010, at the age of 14, she went along to JYP Entertainment's seventh open audition. Still in her school uniform, she sang 'By Myself', a song originally recorded by Tiffany from Girls' Generation. She came second and was offered a place as a trainee. However, she had gone to the audition without telling her parents. It wasn't the career they wanted her to take and she had a difficult task persuading them to let her pursue her dream. Fortunately, she eventually convinced them of her passion for singing and dancing.

On 15 September 2010 Nayeon began life as a trainee at JYP, linking up with Jihyo and Jeongyeon. Nayeon was popular with fellow trainees and staff and her talents were soon recognised as she was given an acting role in the music video for San E's 'You Can't Go'. In 2012 she had a cameo as an aspiring idol student in the TV drama *Dream High 2*, and although she was only on screen for 15 seconds, her dance with Got7's Jinyoung had viewers wondering who that beautiful girl was. She also appeared in a commercial for TN cosmetics where she stood beside Suzy from Miss A – and still garnered attention.

NAYEON

JYP Entertainment realised they had a star on their hands. Nayeon appeared in videos for Got7's 'Girls, Girls, Girls' and Miss A's 'Only You' as well as an ad for *Just Dance 2*. She was an obvious choice for their new girl group 6Mix, and after working so hard to debut, she was distraught when the opportunity disappeared. She lost her motivation for a while, but, reminding herself of how she first felt as a trainee, found the determination to carry on. The *Sixteen* series gave her another opportunity to debut. However, at 20 years old, Nayeon was the oldest of the trainees involved and time was running out.

She appeared on the first individual teaser for *Sixteen*, confirming her status as the leading contender to join the new group with a sharp cover of Taylor Swift's 'Shake It Off' and a line that fans loved: 'I am a girl that is … good to date!' She showed her vocal prowess with a cover of Ariana Grande's 'Santa Tell Me', but when she was demoted to the minor team it demonstrated that even her confidence could be shattered by the intense competition.

Gradually, however, she regained her self-belief. She helped the younger members of her teams, had a great sense of humour, kept morale up, and sang and danced like a professional. JYP recognised this and described her as someone he felt he could now trust in any group. The public felt the same with the girl who described herself as resembling the Pokémon character Squirtle always finishing high in the rankings. Nayeon's place in Twice never seemed in doubt and it was no shock when she was first choice for the new group.

Nayeon is Twice's 'centre' – a K-pop term for the most prominent member in group photographs and choreography. Particularly in the early days, it was Nayeon whose vocals started each song and who began performances centre stage. She was the lead singer, lead dancer and – as Tzuyu was so young when they debuted – was seen as the 'face of the group'. She is also the eldest, but although throughout *Sixteen* she looked out for the younger trainees, she was not voted leader by the other members. Her sense of fun, her relentless teasing and her excellent *aegyo* skills earned her a different title – that of Fake Maknae, which is the term for a member who acts like she is the youngest of the group.

Her sparkling personality is a feature of Twice's variety show performances. At the start Nayeon and Dahyun were the extroverts in a group full of shy young girls. Nayeon showed she was up for anything; always ready to dance, have fun with the hosts and show *aegyo* on demand. Among Once, favourite moments were her rapping appearance on *Idol Room* when she took the name MC Rail, the way she teased JYP when they appeared together on *Knowing Bros* and when she brought the *Running Man* team to their knees by reciting her acrostic poem in the most adorable fashion ever.

When she wasn't being funny, she was being cute (and often both at the same time). She became known for her smile, which was all the more fetching on account of the two front teeth that were slightly longer than the rest. Once took to calling her Bunny and, being Nayeon, she embraced the joke. She has a rabbit soft toy called Kkaengi with which she not only has conversations, but also makes the other members speak to as well.

Her personality and looks quickly won over the Korean public. It didn't take much for a Nayeon meme to go viral: her momentary eye-smile-wink combo in the beginning of the 'Like Ooh Aah' video, the face she pulled while eating ice after a 'Dance the Night Away' music show win or the fan sign video where she wiggled the ears on her bunny hat – all amassed thousands of views.

It isn't just the public who adore her, Nayeon is so popular with other idols she's become known as the Nation's Best Friend. She has been close to Blackpink's Jennie and Jisoo ever since their trainee days. She is in regular contact with Yeri from Red Velvet and lists GFriend's Sowon, Laboum's Solbin and Bambam from Got7 (she used to buy him milk when they were trainees together at JYP) as good friends.

Her real best friends, though, are the eight members of Twice and she isn't embarrassed to call them her soulmates. They call her Nasoong (derived from the Korean word for peach) or use Jihyo's own nickname for herself, Nabongs. In 2019 Nayeon told *Buzzfeed*, 'We talk to each other a lot, everything from small talk to deep conversation. We depend on each other through every hardship.' She spends the most time with Momo (a pairing often known as the 'Peach Sisters') but named Chaeyoung as the friend she goes to when she is having a hard time. Equally, she recognises her role as the senior member, looks after the others and is always there to help with their problems.

The friendship Once love most is the one they call 2Yeon – Nayeon and Jeongyeon, who have known each other since they were 14. Nayeon remembers Jeongyeon being quiet when they first met and feeling a little scared of her, but they soon became friends. They attended high school together (along with RM from BTS) and trained side by side for five years. Since Twice's debut fans have watched them tease, bicker, laugh, hug and indulge in some crowd-pleasing flirting together on stage.

Nayeon also has a special friend. In November 2017 she adopted a Pomeranian puppy. She spent three days trying to come up with a name, but it only took a few seconds for Chaeyoung to suggest Kookeu. The name came from the end of the line that Jihyo sings in 'Likey' (and is also Korean for cookies and ice cream) and totally suited the adorable little bundle of fur.

Kookeu is a regular on Twice's V LIVE and even appeared (alongside Momo's Boo) on the TV show *Incredible Dogs*.

For all the fun that Nayeon brings to the group, her performance skills are invaluable, too. For the rookie group Twice, her confidence and vocal stability were a major asset. She proved she could be relied upon to provide the opening verse as well as the chorus, bridge and even ad libs. In fact, with her high range and bubbly style, Nayeon has often found herself with more lines than main vocalist Jihyo. She provides the backbone of 'Cheer Up', 'Knock, Knock' and 'Heart Shaker' and does a stalwart if repetitive job on 'I'm Gonna be a Star'! However, she is versatile, as evidenced by *More and More*, where she finds a real swagger and even raps.

Although none of the group has so far released solo recordings, Nayeon seems the most likely. In December 2019 she uploaded a solo cover of Ariana Grande's 'Santa Tell Me' (which she performed on *Sixteen*) with a typically sweet Christmas message saying, 'This video is nothing special, but I prepared it for Once.' The video has over ten million views.

Nayeon has also taken advantage of the opportunity to progress her songwriting. Her first was '24/7' on *Twicetagram*, a joint effort with Jihyo about staying positive when every day seems the same. She followed that by writing 'Rainbow' on *Feel Special* where *Billboard* remarked on the song's 'infectious, empowering lyrics', noting the subtle metaphor she used of walking across a rainbow to the purple line. On *More and More* she wrote 'Make Me Go', a song totally suited to the more mature concept. She was inspired by a scene in a horror movie she watched on a plane during their US tour and thought it would be cool for members to show that aspect of the group.

As a lead dancer, Nayeon is integral to the group's dance performances (the Marilyn Monroe move in the choreography of 'Like Ooh-Aah' was her idea). Having learned ballet as a child she has good flexibility, although due to a car accident in her youth she has a weak left leg. This limits her ability to perform some of the more powerful moves and on a few occasions she has been seen to stumble.

As a visual, though, Nayeon is faultless. Her features – small face, straight eyebrows, thin, high nose and plump lips – are the definition of Korean beauty. When out and about, the often-bespectacled Nayeon usually prefers comfortable and casual wear in muted colours that give off a girl-next-door vibe, but even without make-up she is stunning. Very few idols dare venture in front of cameras totally bare-faced, but Nayeon has a reputation for doing so and showing her smooth and flawless skin.

Of course, she looks great on stage and in Twice videos. She manages to shine in frayed denim shorts and a t-shirt, but she has also worn memorable outfits such as the yellow tartan skirt in 'Like Ooh Ahh', the black dress and red cropped sweater combination in 'Knock Knock' and the red velvet crop top of 'What is Love?'. Her cosplay is great fun, whether she's dressing up as a gorgeous red devil, the geeky Mia from *Princess Diaries* (even approved by author Meg Cabot in a tweet) or the shaggy-haired character Old Boy (from a Korean movie she had never seen, but Chaeyoung said was awesome!).

With the occasional variation (including a blonde bob wig for the 'Feel Special' photoshoot), Nayeon's long, dark brown hair has been her go-to style since Twice's debut. Then in April 2020 she surprised everyone with a short bob – then shocked people again by explaining that she did it because she wanted to give her hair to the hospital!

Even after five years Nayeon is still the bright, friendly and vivacious performer that we first met in *Sixteen*. While many K-pop fans appreciate her stunning beauty, Once have also grown to value her contribution to Twice's music and dance, and to appreciate the way she looks after and entertains the group. They will always have a special place in their heart for their Bunny.

16

JEONGYEON

Stage name: Jeongyeon (pronounced
   Chon-yun)
Birth name: Yoo Kyung-wan (legally changed to
   Yoo Jeong-yeon)
Nicknames: Yoo Jangoo, Tajo (ostrich in
   Korean), No Jam-hyung (elder brother)
Lovely name: Jeongvely
Twice colour: Yellow-green
Nationality: Korean
Position: Lead vocalist
Date of birth: 1 November 1996
Zodiac sign: Scorpio
Blood type: O
Height: 168cm (5ft 6in)

When Twice made their debut, Jeongyeon stood out. She was
the only one with short hair, and she was enigmatic, chic and
cast as the girl-crush member of the group. Once would soon
discover that she was also funny and warm-hearted, but to some

she initially came across as more 'boyish' than the others. This wasn't the first time Twice's lead vocalist had been labelled a 'tomboy', though. She was born Yoo Kyung-wan and, although it was a gender-neutral name, her classmates perceived it as 'unfeminine', which led to her being bullied at school. So in the third grade, when she was around 10 years old, she legally changed her name to Jeong-yeon.

However, this is not to say her childhood was unhappy. She was born in Suwon, a city close to Seoul, where her father was a renowned chef at the Seoul Plaza Hotel (having once been the private chef of former president Kim Dae-jung) and her mother ran a Japanese restaurant. With busy parents, Jeongyeon and her two older sisters spent much of their time with their grand-mother. In the *Twice: Seize the Light* documentary, Jeongyeon tearfully recalled how her grandmother had wanted her to fulfil her dream of becoming a singer but had sadly passed away before that dream had come true.

Jeongyeon was not the only one in the family with show-business ambitions. The middle sister, Seungyeon, won the Best Looks prize at the SM Young Adult Best Competition in 2005 and joined SM Entertainment as a trainee. At the company she trained alongside Red Velvet, but after seven years she gave up her musical ambitions and left to pursue a career in acting. Meanwhile, Jeongyeon had followed in her sister's footsteps. Slightly overweight as a child, she attended aerobic classes in a bid to lose weight and gained a passion for dance. She failed in her first attempt to join JYP, and even considered a career as a professional drummer, as she played traditional Korean drums. However, she auditioned again in March 2010 and found herself receiving offers from both SM and JYP on the same day. There was no dilemma: she only ever wanted to join JYP Entertainment.

When she began life as a trainee, of the eventual members of Twice only Jiyho was already at the company. Jihyo was delighted to meet her and her first greeting was apparently, 'You are the same age as me. We must be friends!' (although in the *Seize the Light* documentary she added to the story, saying that it was three months before she spoke to her again). Jeongyeon also remembers attending the following year's audition, when Nayeon was selected. She was struck by how pretty Nayeon was and, although the newcomer was quiet at first, they soon become friends too. The three were the core of the proposed 6Mix and worked towards their debut, but when that was aborted, Jeongyeon, like the others, was frustrated and de-motivated. She took a part-time job and seriously considered pursuing a career in a bakery.

Then came *Sixteen*. Jeongyeon was the final contestant to be given a teaser video, but she immediately made an impression. With her short black hair and black-and-white leather jacket she looked the epitome of cool and became an instant favourite with viewers. JYP himself was clearly enamoured of the 20-year-old, describing her as having a fascinating aura. Jeongyeon built on this with her saxophone performance in the first task and her natural poise in front of the camera in the photoshoot challenge.

Sixteen was no walk in the park, though, even for someone who seemed as confident as Jeongyeon. In her meeting with her sister Seungyeon, she broke down in tears under the pressure. It was after that, in the one-on-one challenge, that she really stunned viewers with a cover of Lady Gaga's 'Applause'. She proved she could do wild and crazy just as well as cool and chic, and still keep her vocals stable. Right up until the last episode, Jeongyeon might have been unsure of her place in Twice, but the audience and JYP staff had little doubt. She was a born star.

When Twice debuted, Jeongyeon would announce herself as the member 'in charge of girl crush'. It suited the 'tomboy' style she presented. She wore light make-up and wasn't seen in a dress, but with a small face and long legs – two essential elements of Korean beauty – she was popular with the public. Her girl-crush vibe continued in their variety shows. Jeongyeon established a dorky reputation and a good sense of humour. She pulled hilarious 'unimpressed' expressions, showed off an ungainly (but very funny) 'ostrich dance', had a running joke where she would shy away from being kissed by other members (especially Sana) and immediately cringed or buried her head in a member's lap after reluctantly displaying *aegyo*.

She was invited to appear solo on *Muscle Queen Project*, where she was paired with R'n'B singer Insooni (who was almost 40 years her senior) to execute exercises and a music performance. She then joined the team of popular TV survival show *Running Man*. Unfortunately, she was kicked by a horse in a freak accident and couldn't complete the task, but fans had seen enough to confirm that she was not only sweet, but brave and determined, too.

This was more evidence that Jeongyeon wasn't actually particularly cool or aloof. The other members had already seen her caring qualities. It emerged that in their dorm she was the mother figure; looking after them, cleaning up and nagging them all to tidy their rooms. This was also evident in video clips of fan meetings and award shows, where Once noticed it was Jeongyeon who checked the group were all safe, attended to any injuries and was even alert for wardrobe malfunctions – holding down the hem of members' skirts on a number of occasions.

Jeongyeon's caring side was also evident away from Twice. When she managed to find time outside their ridiculously busy schedule, she was often seen at an animal sanctuary where she helped look after abandoned cats and dogs. She even encouraged other members to come along and succeeded in enlisting the help of Tzuyu and Momo. At home, Jeongyeon had two dogs of her own: Bbosong, a white Pomeranian, and Nanan, a poodle. Sadly, in 2019, after a year's illness in which all the group visited her at the animal hospital, Bbosong died. Days later, at a concert in Bangkok, Jeongyeon broke down in tears during the ballad 'After Moon'. It was a moment that touched her fellow members and Once, who all showed their support.

In the vote for group leader Jeongyeon came second to Jihyo, and she is clearly well liked by all the members. Her up-and-down relationship with Nayeon, full of bickering and hugs, has been well documented by 2Yeon watchers on fan forums, but the pair have known each other for many years and their friendship runs deep. Momo was her long-time roommate and the two even shared a bed in their original dorm. She shares a love of Lego with Mina and although in public she makes a mock show of rebuffing Sana's affection, the two are often seen hanging out together. Jeongyeon also teams up with Chaeyoung in No Jam Brothers.

Just how close Jeongyeon feels to all the members was demonstrated when she bought them each a $500 black necklace as a surprise gift on the group's third anniversary. It was a generous present and her explanation – they were all struggling to keep up with the hectic schedule and she wanted to give them strength – was touching.

Although she gets on really well with Hyojung from the girl group Oh My Girl, Jeongyeon tends to struggle when asked to name her celebrity friends outside Twice. However, she does have a celebrity as her best friend – her sister Seungyeon. After leaving SM Entertainment, Seungyeon became an actress and her popularity coincided with the rise of Twice. In 2015 she rose to fame in the reality show *We Got Married* and her subsequent performance in *Six Flying Dragons* won her the New Star Award at the SBS Drama Awards. The high-profile sisters were now in demand. They took a trip together for the reality series *We Are Siblings* and for six months co-hosted the music show *Inkigayo* (along with actor Kim Min Suk), which won them a Newcomer Award at the SBS Entertainment Awards. On their first programme Seungyeon joined Twice on stage to perform 'Cheer Up'. Her training at SM served her well, and her singing and dancing impressed fans who rated her good enough to be Twice's tenth member.

The sisters also duetted on a song for *My Dream Class*, a short movie in which Seungyeon starred. The track, called 'Like a Star', showed off Jeongyeon's soft but strong vocals and gave her many more lines than she usually has on Twice recordings. When her voice is exposed – especially her verse in 'Like a Fool', a fabulous high note in 'One in a Million' and when she sang Jihyo's part in 'My Headphones On' at the *Twiceland* concert – Once are fullsome in their praise of Jeongyeon's singing talent.

Although she doesn't often have many lines, Jeongyeon has begun to contribute to songs by writing lyrics. Her first credit came with 'Love Line' on *Twicetagram* (according to Nayeon this was about Jeongyeon's first love). She also wrote 'Lalala' and teamed up with Chaeyoung to provide the lyrics for 'Sweet Talker'. After that song became a fan favourite, she said she'd like to write a summer song in the style of 'Dance the Night Away'. Once didn't have to wait long – enlisting the rapper's help again, she came up with 'Sweet Summer Day', a perfect sun-drenched accompaniment to their tropical bop.

Jeongyeon's visuals have delighted fans since their debut and, despite having to play boyish roles in many of the videos, she continues to shine. Her puppet moves were spot on when she played Pinocchio in 'TT'; she looked stunning in male roles in 'What is Love?' (including evading Sana's attempted kiss in the *Ghost* parody); and was super-cool as a skater girl in 'Likey'. And all the time her hair was still short, whether it was in a bowl cut, with bangs, curls or a half ponytail, it fascinated Once. It went from the flaming red of debut through shades of brown before she emerged as a blonde for the 'What is Love?' comeback in 2017. Perhaps most iconic, though, was the amazing bright aqua-blue hair she presented in May 2018. Only Jeongyeon could carry off an outrageous colour with such class. Many Once were so astonished they missed the fact that this was the longest her hair had been since *Sixteen*.

'Dance the Night Away' was a watershed moment for Jeongyeon. For the first time she looked ultra-feminine. In the video her hair (back to brown) was long and braided, she actually wore a dress – and she looked stunning. 'Yes or Yes' followed, with Jeongyeon given more lines than normal and she had a more central role in the video, playing the suave chauffeur and confidently leading a dance break in her memorable yellow tartan skirt. By 'Fancy' some said her dancing skills had stepped up, but others argued that she was just being noticed now with her long dark hair that fell halfway down her back. As the other members began to look less cutesy, Jeongyeon found herself heading in the other direction, performing more *aegyo* and looking sweet. 'These days,' she said in *Seize the Light*, 'our fans say, "We don't have a girl crush on Jeongyeon – she's too cute!".'

In May 2019, Jeongyeon announced at a concert in Seoul that it was her last day with long hair. When Once asked why, her answer was simple: 'Because I want to.' Once didn't mind. By now they were all aware that there is a whole lot more than a hair style that goes into making Jeongyeon extra special.

17

MOMO

Stage name: Momo (pronounced Mo-mo)
Birth name: Momo Hirai
Nicknames: Peach (Momo is Japanese for 'Peach'), Moguri, Racoon, Dancing Momochine
Lovely name: Movely
Twice colour: Pink
Nationality: Japanese
Position: Main dancer, vocalist, rapper
Date of birth: 9 November 1996
Zodiac sign: Scorpio
Blood type: A
Height: 162cm (5ft 4in)

Momo is Twice's dance machine. She is lithe and energetic, and brings power and style to the group's choreography, and yet the girl from Japan was nearly the one who got away – only saved by the intervention of JYP himself. Many say it was the best decision he has ever made.

As traumatic a journey as all the other members had on *Sixteen*, none suffered quite as much as Momo, for whom the process was a stressful and emotional rollercoaster ride. When she appeared (without bangs) on the series' eighth teaser, viewers got a tantalising glimpse of this Japanese trainee who was already being feted as the Dancing Queen. Momo's skills were there for all to see as she began the competition, but she struggled to impress with her stage presence and her vocals and so found herself in the minor group and in danger of elimination.

In a despondent call home to her sister, Momo questioned whether she even wanted to debut. Nevertheless, she improved in each challenge – a mesmerising dance to Ariana's 'Problem' in the one-on-ones and a superb routine to JYP's own 'Swing Baby' alongside Chaeyoung and Jiwon were highlights. However, due to the viewers' vote, JYP reluctantly eliminated Momo. It was a bombshell that shocked and upset everyone, especially the other Japanese contestants, because they knew just how talented Momo was.

Momo was devastated, too. At first she couldn't bear to tell her family as she felt she had let them down, but having talked to them she resolved to stay at the company and work as hard as she could. Two weeks later, along with fellow eliminated contestants Chaeyeon and Eunsuh, she uploaded a dance cover of 2PM's 'My House'. It was this work ethic and determination that JYP alluded to when he shocked viewers by adding Momo as the last member of Twice in the dramatic conclusion to *Sixteen*.

Debuting was the fulfilment of long-held ambition. Momo had been dancing since she was a three-year-old growing up in Kyōtanabe, near Kyoto, Japan. Her mother inspired in Momo a love of K-pop, especially of singer and dancer Rain, and female singer Lee Hyori, and aged 11 (a cute) Momo appeared in the video for Korean singer Lexy's 'Ma People'. In 2011, Momo, along with her elder sister Hana and two friends, entered the talent show *Superstar K* as a dance troupe called Barbie, but were eliminated in the qualifying round. Later that year, however, JYP saw a video they had uploaded and invited Momo and Hana to their Japanese audition. Although Momo passed, sadly Hana didn't make the cut and the younger sister had to make the trip to Korea herself.

It wasn't easy for Momo. She was only 15 years old and barely spoke any Korean. However, she did have a fellow Japanese trainee friend in Sana, who joined JYP on the very same day in 2012. Shy and unable to communicate with many of the other trainees, Momo concentrated hard on her training. She soon gained experience with cameos in music videos, including Junho's 'Feel', Got7's 'Stop Stop It' and Wooyoung's 'R.O.S.E.'. With JYP seemingly making plans for an all-Japanese girl group, the future looked bright, but when that failed to materialise, at least being put forward for *Sixteen* was some compensation. She was beautiful, a great dancer and would appeal to the Japanese market. What could possibly go wrong?

Any fallout over Momo's inclusion in Twice was blown away at their debut. Since *Sixteen* she had lost seven kilos at the company's request and was in fabulous shape. Her hair was now long and yellow-blonde with full bangs and she was given the sexiest outfits of all the group, including the black-net swimsuit and the clip-pants. She also took centre stage for a dance break that contained impossible-to-forget hair flicks. Over the run of promotions through 2017 – especially on 'Cheer Up', 'Likey' and 'Touchdown' – every time Momo took up position Once knew something special was coming. Her moves were vibrant and powerful.

Momo is undoubtedly the most ripped member of the group. A daily routine of weights, sit-ups and stretches (she reportedly does 50 planks three times a day) gives her defined abs and toned shoulders. These are shown off proudly in the crop tops and off-the-shoulder dresses the group wear regularly, and while her debut image took some beating, Once purred over her yellow *La La Land* dress in the 'What is Love?' video, the black tube dress with chains she wore in the 'Fancy' video and the floral ruffled dress of 'More and More'.

After stunning fans with her blonde hair in 'Like Ooh Ahh', Momo disappointed many by immediately adopting varying shades of brown for subsequent comebacks. She still managed to rock waves, space buns and pigtails, but in the summer of 2017 surprised everyone by unveiling shoulder-length electric-blue locks. Other hair transformations that went down well with Once were the dark bob of 'What is Love?', the deep black look of 'Fancy' and the 2020 return to blonde, but nothing matched the moment in 2019 when a teaser for 'Feel Special' featured Momo with no bangs – the first time since the debut that her forehead had been revealed! Such was the amazement, #Momo trended at number one on Twitter in the USA even though Apple had just released their new iPhone!

After 'Heart Shaker' Momo's dance breaks featured less often in Twice choreography, but there were plenty of opportunities for Once to see her killer moves. JYP released videos of Momo dancing to 2PM's Jun.K's solo track 'Think About You' and also uploaded official videos of her performing the choreography to many of the singles. Soon after Twice's debut, Momo took part in the dance competition series *Hit the Stage*. There her bloody vampire dance raised pulses and her haunting portrayal (alongside Mina) of an abusive relationship set to Beyoncé's 'Dangerous in Love' provoked discussion of the theme in Korea.

Momo's special stages at Twice concerts and a number of performances on TV shows, often with the best dancers from other groups, continued to showcase her talents and in 2019 she was reunited on the dancefloor with her sister. Hana, who is now a dancer with That crew in Japan, impressed Once by matching her sister's flexibility and control as they danced to Imagine Dragons' 'Believer'. Momo did that while on holiday, because she was bored. Dancing is her release and V LIVE has captured so many of her cover dances, including highly complex boy band choreography.

How good is she? On the *Idol Radio* show, top choreographer Lia Kim named Momo as the best dancer in K-pop. She described her as 'a dancer sent down from the gods' and marvelled at Momo's ability to learn a routine after watching it once, then add her own touches to make it even better.

When dancing Momo is confident and out-there, and her toned abs and defined muscles give her a powerful presence. Those who work with her at JYP know a different Momo – a shy young woman who loves her Barbies and teddy bears and is forever hugging and stroking the other members. Momo has spoken of her problems with social anxiety and shyness, and it is unsurprising that she has few close friends in the K-pop world. She is, however, very popular within the group. The J-line have always been a tight unit and she is especially close to Sana, who has been by her side since their first day as trainees. The two even took a trip to Hawaii together in May 2019. Jeongyeon has been her roommate since before debut, Nayeon was invited to Momo's family home in Japan during a break and in a radio broadcast Tzuyu gave Momo a 'friendship award' for always being there for her when she was bored.

In the Twice dorm, Momo managed to acquire the reputation of being a bit of an airhead, often seeming distracted or spaced out. Members have teased her for not knowing her blood type and for melting her Barbie's hair by using a curling iron on it.

Expending so much energy in dance rehearsals also enables her to indulge in her other favourite activity – eating! 'If I work hard, I can eat delicious things,' is her mantra. Trying Korean delicacies really helped her settle when she was new to the country, and she especially grew to love *jokbal* (spicy pigs' trotters) and *budae Jjigae* (sausage stew).

Momo is another of Twice's dog-loving posse. The only problem is that she is allergic to them, often finding rashes on her arms or her face after she has touched them, but it doesn't seem to stop her. She grew up in a family who raised three Jack Russell puppies and always listed them – Lucky, Pudding and Petco – in the thanks on Twice albums. In May 2002 Momo went on V LIVE at two in the morning to introduce her five-month-old Norwich Terrier puppy, called Boo, named after her favourite *Monsters Inc.* character.

Through her performances and appearances on V LIVE and *Twice TV* variety shows, Momo has become many fans' bias. She is capable of being completely lovable – for example, on the sketch show *Gag Concert*, when she was told to clean the house, she pretended to be a Japanese robot, repeating 'Made in Japan' in English. It was a priceless moment. However, for all she is funny and cute (and has the sweetest sneeze!), it was part of a rap from *Sixteen*, in which she rapped the words 'Pink Lamborghini', that really went viral. Some liked the way she pronounced the words, while others thought it seemed so un-Momo like. Jihyo did an impression of her saying it in the first episode of *Twice TV*, a 10-minute loop of those two words appeared on YouTube and, for Once, the phrase is forever associated with her.

There was one person who fell completely for Momo's variety show charms. Heechul of boy band Super Junior first encountered Momo as a host on *Knowing Bros*, but it was their meeting on *Weekly Idol* in 2016 that caught the public's imagination. In one part of the show the guests competed to see who could best raise Heechul's heart rate. When it was Momo's turn, she performed her best *aegyo* and imitated the 'Nico Nico Nii' catchphrase from the anime *Love Live! School Idol Project*. It sent Heechul's heartbeat soaring. Momo hadn't only won the task, she'd won his heart!

Heechul became a regular guest at Twice concerts and his sweet interactions with Momo on future variety shows and Instagram clips (one where they appeared to be holding hands just before the filming began) were closely monitored by Once. In August 2019 Heechul was moved to deny they were in a relationship, but a year later it was confirmed that the two stars had been friends but were now dating. In past times romantic relationships between idols have often created a rift between performers and fans, who sometimes saw it as a betrayal. Momo and Heechul were understandably concerned about the reaction to the news. Although there were some raised eyebrows at Heechul being 13 years her senior, Once and most of the K-pop world seemed genuinely pleased for the couple, and both idols appreciated the support and love they received from fans.

Momo has always been a favourite with Once, though, and their special nickname for her is Moguri. *Noguri* is the Korean word for racoon and Momo's big eyes, cuddliness, love of food and other antics led them to associate her with the animal. She has also become their V LIVE Queen, taking any opportunity – often in the back of a taxi – to talk to fans. In August 2019 she delighted international fans by singing Queen's 'Bohemian Rhapsody' and showing off her piano playing, but she had already gone down in Once history a few months earlier when she undertook a mighty seven-hour V LIVE broadcast.

Momo's dancing credentials are beyond question, but she contributes so much more to the group. She choreographs dance breaks and helps other members learn the dances, supplies vocals and raps to many songs, provides stunning visuals, is entertaining on screen and is a great friend to the other members. With hindsight, JYP's decision to bring Momo back from *Sixteen* elimination now seems like some kind of divine inspiration.

18

SANA

Stage name: Sana (pronounced Sa-na)
Birth name: Sana Minatozaki
Nicknames: Snake, Sanaconda, Shiba Inu
Lovely name: Savely
Twice colour: Purple
Nationality: Japanese
Position: Vocalist, lead dancer
Date of birth: 29 December 1996
Zodiac sign: Capricorn
Blood type: B
Height: 163cm (5ft 4in)

Even those who never listened to K-pop knew about the 'Sha Sha Sha' girl. It was Sana who sang the line from 'Cheer Up' that boosted the group to stardom, but that was no coincidence. There was something about the girl from Japan that was funny, cute and appealing and perfect for a three-second clip – as Once discovered, she was a one-woman meme machine …

It was this instant appeal which kicked off Sana's K-pop career back when she was just 14 years old. While shopping in Osaka, a large city in Japan, she was spotted by a JYP scout and asked if she would like to attend an audition. Sana grew up in Japan during the first Korean Wave. She liked Girls' Generation, Kara and other successful K-pop acts, and was already an accomplished dancer who attended EXPG, a dance studio where many J-pop idols had trained.

The JYP audition was the very next day and Sana performed the choreography for 'Mr. Taxi' by Girls' Generation. Although she is now embarrassed by it, Once love the short clip of her audition and the other members regularly tease her about it or make her repeat the dance as a penalty for losing a game. JYP liked it enough to offer her a place as a trainee in Seoul. Before she let her only child go off to Korea, Sana's mother took her to watch a 2PM concert. When Sana confirmed that was what she wanted to do, her parents sent her off with their best wishes.

In April 2012, at the age of 15, Sana moved to Korea to begin training. She knew no Korean but picked it up quickly and was soon acting as an interpreter for other trainees, including her new best friend, Momo. However, Sana did admit on a variety show that she sometimes pretended not to understand Korean – especially when she was being told off!

The company noted her talent and looks, and in 2014 she was given a starring role as a waitress eyed up by each of the group in Got7's music video for 'A'. She was in line for a place in the all-Japanese group JYP was putting together, but when 6Mix lost a member close to debut Sana was the replacement. Then, as both groups became casualties of JYP's rethink, she found herself among the *Sixteen* contenders.

Viewers had no idea what was in store for them – in her *Sixteen* teaser Sana performed cartwheels in her cheerleader's outfit. The other contenders sang and danced in the first round, but she gave a cookery lesson (she even made a point of explaining that she didn't use organic vegetables in the spring rolls), but she soon proved there was more to her than eccentricity: not only was she fun and bubbly, but she could dance, sing and looked amazing in her 'Sailor Moon' outfit in the photoshoot challenge.

Of course, *Sixteen* eventually challenged everyone. Sana's moment came in the confrontation over dance practice with Dahyun and Minyoung, which made her angry, but also brought her to tears. Suddenly the dizzy, laughter-loving girl turned serious, dealing with the situation calmly and respectfully. She went on to be a complete star in the variety tasks (capsizing her own inflatable in her excitement) and won votes ahead of established Korean trainees. Jihyo told JYP that if he watched her variety performances he'd find she lived up to every one of his expectations. In the final challenge, she even rapped pretty well on 'Do it Again', although when Twice eventually recorded the song the part was given to Chaeyoung. If *Sixteen* was supposed to discover stars, it had struck gold with Sana.

The video for Twice's debut single 'Like Ooh Ahh' made it clear that Sana was the 'funny' member of the group. She could laugh at herself as she tried to mimic Mina and Momo's flexibility or fell on her backside when the others jumped off the bus so coolly. But she was also adorable in her pigtails. JYP had successfully shown her endearing charisma, but what happened next was totally unplanned.

'Shy, shy, shy' – Sana's three words in 'Cheer Up' – ran through the internet like wildfire. At first she was upset because she had worked so hard to get the English pronunciation right and now everyone was laughing at her by singing, 'Sha, sha, sha'. Only later did she realised the affection with which it was being repeated. JYP were quick to realise its meme potential and when they promoted the song they introduced a dance move that Sana pulled off with added super *aegyo*.

Having made such a huge impression, Sana now began to establish her own image in the group. With her wide eyes and beaming smile she was capable of looking incredibly sweet but she could also do wild and alluring, especially in the special stages in live concerts. In fact, she could do both at the same time and was soon being heralded as the 'cutie-sexy' member as a whole series of gifs showing her on stage, attempting to wink, wearing bunny ears, looking like a Shiba Inu puppy (a famous Japanese dog breed) or just sleepy were eagerly shared online.

While the general public still thought of her as the 'Shy, shy, shy' girl, Once had moved on, especially when an appearance on *Knowing Bros* threw up another adorable meme. In the TV show the members played a game that involved wearing noise-cancelling headphones and passing on a message by reading each other's lips. Sana was required to guess what Jeongyeon was saying and worked it out correctly, but it was the extreme cuteness of the way she said 'cheese *kimbap*' that prompted the clip to be viewed thousands of times.

Sana's off-stage antics are a constant source of entertainment for Once. They love watching her bright, outgoing personality on V LIVEs and variety shows. They laugh at her clumsiness, as she constantly knocks things over and trips, and they collect her ultra-cute klutzy expressions such as 'Green tea is green', 'The desk was just a desk' and 'It's like carbonated water without carbonisation'. Every detail that emerges about Sana seems to make her more lovable: the way she puts her fists up when she gets angry, her random interjections of 'Ohyo Ohyo' (she says it means nothing and is just something she likes to say), how she buys new shoes when she's stressed and her ecstatic reaction on being told she resembled Harry Potter when she wore her geeky glasses. Most of all, Once treasure her interactions with other members. She is so friendly and tactile, always kissing or trying to kiss the others – it's hard to believe, but Jihyo says that when she drinks alcohol she becomes even more affectionate and full of *aegyo*. Once jokingly call her 'the snake', implying she bestows her affection indiscriminately and will flit from member to member.

In the Twice dorm, they've learned to live with Sana's exuberance. They join in, encourage her, tease her and sometimes just ignore her. She originally shared the large room with Mina, Jihyo and Nayeon, with whom she has now been friends for many years. Sana is also part of Twice's J-Trinity and has a special bond with Momo and Mina – her distraught reaction when Momo was eliminated in *Sixteen* showed just how close they are – and in April 2020, Sana and Momo celebrated eight years of friendship. However, despite being together 24/7 for all that time, they never seem to tire of each other, even taking trips together when there are breaks in their schedule. Sana also remains close to Mina and felt her absence deeply in 2019. During this period Sana had a photograph of Mina as her phone screensaver and would carry a penguin plushie to remind audiences (as if they needed reminding!) of her missing friend.

In Korea as well as Japan and around the world, Once have taken Sana to their hearts. In Korean the word 'sana' is part of the verb meaning 'to live' and fans there coined the phrase '*Sana eobsin, sana mana*', which roughly translates as, 'Without Sana, there is no life.' International fans then came up with their own version: 'No Sana no life' (possibly inspired by *No Game No Life*, the series of light novels and TV series by Yū Kamiya). It is a perfect way of describing how much she means to them and fan chants and banners proclaiming the sentiment have become unmissable at Twice concerts.

The intense public scrutiny of being a K-pop idol is the one thing that managed to wipe the smile from Sana's face. May 2019 saw the abdication of the Japanese Emperor Akihito and the end of the era in which Sana had been born. Sana used the Twice Instagram account to say she was sad to see that era end and to congratulate Heisei (the name given to Akihito after his death). Considering the contentious history between the nations, many Koreans considered the comments insensitive, especially as Sana was a Japanese member of a Korean group. The criticism clearly affected Sana, but she was brave enough to face up to it and at the end of that month, at the *Twicelights* concert in Seoul, she delivered a tearful speech thanking Once and others who had supported her through the controversy.

While bewitching fans with her offstage personality, Sana is also an integral part of recordings, videos and performances. Like all the members, Sana has fans who believe her vocals deserve more lines in Twice songs. Her briefly heard honey-coated voice certainly adds another texture to many of the tracks and her vocals really shine in songs like 'What is Love?' and 'Like a Fool'. However, it was in her 'Feel Special' chorus that fans heard Sana sing with real passion and the quality of her vocals surprised many who hadn't noticed her before. She has also proved herself a gifted dancer and this, added to her unyielding smile and a seemingly endless supply of seductive facial expressions, gives her a strong stage presence.

Sana is one of the most popular members of the group, not only in Japan but also in Korea (in 2019 she was rated fifteenth among favourite K-pop idols – the highest-rated non-Korean) and internationally. Throughout her time with Twice, her stunning visuals have been a major factor in her popularity. With her cute-sexy style she always adds something to the cheerleader and girly outfits. She looked so good in the 'Likey' blue tartan dress and the 'Fancy' pink-and-white Chanel outfit that some compared her to a Barbie doll, and she can carry off super-sexy, too, as demonstrated by the sequin dress, black leather jacket and thigh-high red boots of 'Feel Special'.

In each comeback fans can rely on Sana to reveal a new look. In the first 18 months after debut she went through at least 10 hair colours, including an orange, red and pink-sunset combination, platinum blonde (Sana's own favourite) and the silver she revealed at an LG Twins baseball match. She didn't stop there, either, trying purple tips, a bright pink and, when she finally had her hair cut short in 2020, orange.

Sana's love for the other Twice members and Once is clear in the positivity and affection she brings to every aspect of the group. In June 2020, she told the *Soompi* K-pop website: 'I've spent a long time with fans, our members, and the staff, and I want to be with them for even longer. There's a saying that nothing is forever, but I want to stay with these people forever.' That can only please Once, because, as their mantra says, 'No Sana no life.'

19

Stage name: Jihyo (pronounced Chi-yo)
Birth name: Park Ji-soo
Nicknames: God-Jihyo, Mic, Thomas
Lovely name: Jively
Twice colour: Apricot
Nationality: Korean
Position: Leader, main vocalist
Date of birth: 1 February 1997
Zodiac sign: Aquarius
Blood type: O
Height: 160cm (5ft 3in)

It takes someone pretty special to be given the nickname 'God'. Read any forum discussing Twice and it won't be long before God-Jihyo appears. What has she done to deserve this? Nothing – she is just herself onstage and offstage; and everything – she is selfless, caring, positive and charming, as well as being a great singer and dancer who looks fabulous. Yet of all the Twice members, Jihyo has had the toughest journey to stardom; one which still throws up obstacles that she determinedly overcomes.

Growing up in Guri, a city just a 20-minute drive from Seoul, the young Park Ji-soo took her first step to becoming an idol back in August 2004. With encouragement from her parents, the eight-year-old entered the Junior Naver child acting star competition and came second. She attracted the attention of JYP Entertainment scouts and in 2005 was invited to become a trainee. Pictures of those early years at JYP show a happy and incredibly cute child who was a favourite of the older trainees, including Jun K, who would debut with 2PM, Jo Kwon of 2AM, who also became a TV presenter, and future Wonder Girl, Sunye.

The average training period for JYP Entertainment trainees is around three years. Jihyo started early, so she expected to spend an extended time as a trainee, but nonetheless she watched other trainees, who joined the company after her, debut in groups such as the Wonder Girls, 2PM and Miss A. Despite being cast (along with Nayeon and boy band Boyfriend) as a face of cosmetic brand Innisfree's teen line, TN, in 2011, Jihyo still found herself waiting and waiting. Only in 2014 did her break finally come, when she was lined up to debut with the new girl group 6Mix. She came so close, only for the window of opportunity to close as JYP changed plans. By the time *Sixteen* came along, she had been a trainee for 10 years – a long time even in the world of K-pop.

Before *Sixteen* began she legally changed her name from Jis-oo to her stage name Jihyo. Everything had to be perfect. Failure was not an option. As she said, 'Because I started [performing] at a very young age, I felt like this is the only thing I could do.' In the series she was a natural on stage, whether singing solo or taking the tough high notes in the group challenges. She was only the fifth oldest, but she cared for all the trainees, not just those in her team, and encouraged her team-mates to keep practising even when they were down. She was extremely popular among the other girls, topping the poll among the contestants, and Sana summed it up when she explained, 'She's just perfect and always thinks about others.'

All of this was even more impressive considering the pressure Jihyo had to cope with during the series. In just the second challenge the photographer called her 'fat' and it was a jibe that stuck and followed her throughout the series and beyond. According to Jihyo's mother, when 6Mix didn't debut the stress caused her to gain more than 10 kilos in a week and she had never lost it. JYP, who clearly thought the world of her, first defended her, but eventually brought the subject up himself. It was a sign of Jihyo's character that she responded by choosing to sing Meghan Trainor's body-positive anthem 'All About That Bass' and knocked it way out of the park. After the final chal-lenge, JYP was forced to admit to her that, 'You are perfect now and ready to debut', and, despite only finishing eighth in the viewers' poll, she was selected for the group.

One of the first things Twice members had to do was choose a spokesperson to make decisions on everything – from what they ate to their living arrangements. JYP emphasised that their leader must be willing to put others before themselves and Jihyo was the obvious candidate: she was humble, but also had the respect of every member; she was caring and nurturing (having had good experience with two sisters, six and 12 years younger than her); and had great speaking skills and authority, helped by having the loudest voice of all the members! Unsurprisingly, she was unanimously voted in as leader.

She soon proved she was worthy of the title as she stepped forward at press conferences, interviews and award shows. She had a steely determination but a soft heart, with the others citing her as the one who teared up the most. In fact, she cried at their first showcase, on their first music show win and, when explaining what the moment meant to her, at the end of their first solo concert. Many Once also shed tears as she said: 'It would be a lie if I said that I had never wanted to give up after 10 years as a trainee. Just a year and a half ago, I came to the concerts of my seniors and sat in the corner imagining how I would perform if I got a chance to be on this stage.'

Fans took to the group's leader from the beginning. They loved her bubbly personality, her vulnerability and her sense of humour. She could pull such cute poses that they called her the 'aegyo queen'. Within the group she became known as a human mic (microphone) due the sheer volume of her voice. She identifies with Jigglypuff, the pink spherical *Pokémon* character with mesmerising eyes, and has also given herself the nickname Thomas, saying she looks like the children's animation character Thomas the Tank Engine — and few could deny her impersonation is funny and pretty accurate!

Within the group Jihyo remains close to Nayeon and Jeongyeon, the members she spent so much time with as a trainee, as well as Sana, who also nearly joined them in 6Mix. Although on rare occasions she has been known to scold them — as the leader, that's her role — they all know she has quite a sense of mischief and regularly pranks her fellow members. Jihyo also has a special relationship with Tzuyu. She looked after the *maknae* who was on her own so far from home and even invited her back to stay with her family when Tzuyu was alone in the dorm.

Jihyo was a central figure as Twice established themselves as a force in K-pop. Her beaming smile was prominent in every performance and those big round eyes made her easy to pick out among unfamiliar faces. As main vocalist, her dependable, strong vocals are a feature of the group's recordings. This is especially evident in live shows, but she also has some unofficial solo recordings to her name. In 2016 she sang (including a duet with Seventeen's DK) on the *King of Mask Singer* show where her romantic and deep tones surprised the panel when she removed her 'ghost' mask and as part of Twice's Melody Project on V LIVE she did several covers, including a beautiful version of Loveholics' 'Butterfly'. In 2020 she returned to the project with a cover of Jang Hye Jin's 'A Late Night of 1994' in which she amazed fans with a previously unheard mature, jazz-tinged singing voice.

Along with Chaeyoung, she was also the first of the group to contribute lyrics for a Twice song as together they wrote 'Eyes Eyes Eyes' for the *Signal* EP. She then joined Nayeon to write '24/7' on *Twicetagram*, before stepping up to write on her own. Each song saw her progress as a songwriter: from 'Ho!', telling of a first date and 'Sunset', a poetic extended metaphor exploring the anguish and addictiveness of love, to 'Girls Like Us', an uplifting song from her own experience which she dedicated to 'Those who are dreaming and having a hard time', and the angry 'Get Loud' on *Feel Special*.

For all the appreciation of Jihyo's performance and leadership skills, for much of her time with Twice she still faced endless criticism over her weight. In a world where every female artist is beyond slender, Jihyo's chubby cheeks and slightly rounded figure first garnered attention during *Sixteen*. Despite a three-month extreme diet before Twice debuted, and the fact that she continued to lose weight long afterwards, many hurtful comments still appeared. In a 2020 interview with *Allure* magazine, she was confident enough to hit back at having to fit into an 'unrealistic' image, insisting she didn't feel the need to be skinny.

Many fans have long been ahead of her, already appreciating the charms of the singer. Jihyo won over fans in her 'Cheer Up' cheerleader outfit, her 'Knock Knock' graffiti dress and her Elsa from *Frozen* costume in 'TT', as well as the more sophisticated pinstripes, suits and dresses of the award shows, but it was the 'Dance the Night Away' era that took the breath away. Her sun-kissed tan and long hair with silver tips perfectly captured the summer vibe and she looked stunning in the white outfits.

For those first few years of Twice, Jiyho wore her hair long – whether fiery red in 'Like Ooh Aah', tied in a ponytail, dyed light with a wavy perm or black with heavy bangs. The first time we saw her with short hair was in autumn 2018. Once reacted enthusiastically to her bob, but when she followed it with the dark off-centre parting to debut 'Fancy' on *M Countdown* the excitement went viral. Looking chic and pretty, Jihyo went blonde for the first time for the *Twicelights* concerts in Japan at the end of 2019, with a pink tint added in April 2020 that ensured she stood out in the group's blonde-line.

Jihyo isn't just popular with the other Twice members and Once. Having spent so long as a trainee, she numbers many idols as friends, including Miss A's Suzy, the Wonder Girls' Sunmi (who joined JYP on the same day as Jihyo), and Nichkun and Taecyeon of 2PM. She does regret hitting Taecyeon with a bag when she was 11, saying he still hasn't forgiven her! She is also close to Sowon, Yerin and Eunha from GFriend, Oh My Girl's Seunghee and Hyewon from Iz★One. However, it is her relationship with former Wanna One singer Kang Daniel that has generated most interest. Although in August 2019 their companies announced they had 'good feelings towards each other', it was reported that they had been dating since January that year. Their schedules restrict the time they can spend together, but all the signs were they were still seeing each other as Kang launched his solo career in 2020.

Once know that Twice's leader has a vulnerable side — she has confessed she has bouts of stage fright that almost prevent her from performing and they have seen the tears she cries on stage. Nevertheless, in January 2020, a dismissive response to a fan's question in an online chat led to quite harsh criticism from some fans. In an unprecedented and candid letter to Once, Jiyho apologised and explained that she had been suffering from anxiety at the time, writing, 'In the future, as long as I'm a celebrity and an idol, there are going to be issues and rumours, but I'm going to do well. I don't want to make you spend precious time, when we can be happy and laugh and smile together, on other [negative] things.'

There is so much to love about Jihyo: her smile and infectious laugh, her vocal ability, the leadership she gives to the group, her alluring dance moves and, of course, those big brown eyes. Among Once, she may not be as popular as some of the other members of the group (the competition is tough), but few don't respect how she wears her heart on her sleeve and what she brings to the group. She is, after all, god-like.

20

Stage name: Mina (pronounced Mee-na)
Birth name: Mina Myoui
Nicknames: Penguin, Minari, Black Swan, Queen
    of Bridges
Lovely name: Mively
Twice colour: Mint green
Nationality: Japanese
Position: Main dancer, vocalist
Date of birth: 24 March 1997
Zodiac sign: Aries
Blood Type: A
Height: 163cm (5ft 4in)

When Mina was forced to take a hiatus from the group in 2019, it revealed how much she is cherished by Once all over the world. The outpouring of love, online and at concerts, was incredible and showed just how much they value their shy and beautiful Japanese Penguin.

Mina famously said she couldn't do the cute expressions and gestures – *aegyo* – expected of K-pop idols. She was being typically modest, because she can pose sweetly as well any of the group. The difference is that Mina really doesn't need to. With her poise, her smile, her demeanour and her charm, she could break any cute-meter without even trying!

Childhood photographs of Mina show she has always had these qualities. She was born in San Antonio, Texas, in the US, but while still a toddler her family returned to Japan, where her father took up a senior position at Osaka University Hospital. Mina and her older brother Kai grew up in Kobe, a city near Osaka on the south coast of Japan's main island, where she attended an elite Catholic private school.

In 2013, a JYP scout came across the 16-year-old Mina as she was shopping in Osaka with her mother. It was the last day of JYP's auditions in Japan, but Mina was eager to attend. She had tried a couple of auditions in the past but wasn't going miss an opportunity to impress such a prestigious company. Of course she was nervous, but she had reason to be confident in her abilities. For 11 years she had trained as a ballerina and she was also familiar with K-pop. Like the other Japanese members, she was the right age to have enjoyed the first wave of K-pop success in Japan. A junior high school friend had introduced her to Girls' Generation and other groups, and they would dance the routines together. She was soon adding to her ballet skills by taking K-pop dance lessons at the Urizip Dance School near Osaka and when the 2012 Golden Disc Awards were held in Osaka (the first time they were held outside South Korea), Mina even got to see Girls' Generation perform live.

Impressed with Mina's singing and dancing ability, JYP offered her a place as a trainee. At first, she said, her parents were opposed to her going to Korea, especially as she was doing so well in her ballet and at school. However, Mina was serious and passionate about her dream of becoming a K-pop idol and convinced them in time to let her take up her place in Seoul in January 2014. There she linked up with Sana and Momo and the other trainees looking to debut in JYP's proposed Japanese group, but when that hit the buffers, Mina, now 18, found herself competing with 15 other hopefuls for a place in Twice.

Mina gave herself a head start in *Sixteen* with a teaser that immediately won over many fans. They were intrigued by this beautiful girl who looked so innocent, spoke softly and had the cutest laugh but turned in a wickedly raunchy dance cover of Britney Spears's 'Breathe on Me'. She did herself no harm either when, in her first interview, she showed her quirky side by choosing ketchup (but, she insisted, it had to be Heinz ketchup) as her treasured item. So far, so good, but there was still the small matter of a reality show to negotiate.

Despite having been a trainee for little over a year, Mina hit the ground running. In answer to the first 'What makes me a star?' task, she showed off her ballet skills with an elegant performance. She transfixed JYP who, to the surprise of her rivals, placed her in the major team. She then consolidated her position with an inspired Snow White Evil Queen concept in the photoshoot and a stunning dance cover of Beyoncé's 'Drunk in Love', which took viewers back to the 'dark sexy' image of the teaser. Unfortunately, as the competition unfolded, JYP questioned Mina's stage presence and she yo-yoed between majors and minors, which didn't help her confidence. Put in a team alongside Jeongyeon and Nayeon, she felt out of her depth and, when she couldn't keep up, broke down in tears.

Her turning point came later in the series when she was placed in a team with the younger Natty and Somi. Admitting she had previously followed the senior trainees, Mina now stepped up as a leader. In performance this brought out a playful, assertive side where she even altered the words of JYP's own 'Who's Your Mama?' to cheekily describe him as her ideal type! Once again, she suffered from nerves in the first song of the last challenge, but then she came back with a strong final performance. Viewers of the series had taken to the quiet Japanese girl with the winning smile and been impressed with her singing and dancing. They voted her into fourth place in the final ranking. As for JYP and his staff, they knew that Mina was not the finished article, but had seen enough potential to know she would be a valuable member of Twice.

There was just something about Mina. That's what so many fans said when they named her as their bias. Many couldn't put their finger on just what it was, but it seemed to be a combination of her introverted nature, her cute expressions, her delicate features, her elegant dance moves and, of course, her amazing looks. After all, this is the girl who went viral just for the way she gracefully got out of a car!

She could carry off the deep red hair of 'Like Ooh Ahh', the full bangs of 'What is Love?' and the blonde locks in 'More and More' (she claimed the other members said she had to dye it as her hair was in too good condition!), and she always looked incredible. She wore outfits that revealed she had the abs of an athlete and the shoulders of a model, and she carried herself with real elegance when dressed in suits or full-length dresses. Once especially loved her light-brown shoulder-length hair, which matched the schooldays looks of 'Cheer Up'; the self-assured Mina of 'Yes or Yes' in black pinafore dress over the blue and red tartan shirt; and the fierce combination of the chic Versace minidresses and the long, high ponytail which she flicked to stunning effect in the 'Fancy' choreography.

Twice's variety show appearances are always going to be stressful for someone as shy as Mina. However, she is confident in her dance skills and uses those to entertain. She performed ballet moves to K-pop hits on *Knowing Bros*, showed her flexibility with a vertical split as she took the 'Like Ooh Ahh' dance break on *Inkigayo*, and later on *Running Man*, surprised Once who saw another side of Mina when she unleashed the most hilarious, dorky dance to Ayo & Teo's viral hit 'Rolex'.

Mina's dance skills are a key element of Twice's performances and concerts to the point where JYP amended her position in the group from lead dancer to a main dancer alongside Momo. In choreographed dances she was always precise, controlled, effortless and elegant, while when the opportunity to freestyle arose, she showed energy and innovation. She really shone in the cover dances performed at special stages in Twice concerts and proved a graceful counterpoint to Momo's power, perhaps most clearly exhibited in the duo's cover of 'Dangerous Love' on the *Hit the Stage* TV show.

Her contribution to Twice doesn't end with her dancing: Mina can sing as well and her soft, soothing voice is keenly picked out by Once in the group's recordings. Given that Twice is a nine-member group, she is trusted with a good number of lines and her choruses in 'Likey' and 'TT', and her parts in songs like 'Ice Cream', 'Three Times a Day' and 'Trick It' really stand out. Indeed, so often is she given the pre-verse or pre-climax parts that Once nicknamed her the 'Queen of Bridges'. From 'Knock Knock' to 'Candy Pop' and from 'One in a Million' to 'Be as One', it is Mina's angelic voice which provides the variation and progression in the song.

Once have other nicknames for Mina. They call her Black Swan because of her ballerina skills and elegance and, like her friends in Twice, they call her Minari. That cute name reflects her personality; she is quiet and reserved but does have a quirky side. Once love to see her poke fun at the others or let out her adorably cute laugh, but their favourite clip is probably of angry Mina, when she threw the sweetest strop after the others didn't listen – or hear her soft voice – as she read out the comments on V LIVE.

On *Sixteen* Mina revealed that she was often called Penguin. Fans don't forget that kind of thing and ever since she has been inundated with penguin-themed gifts. She is often seen in a penguin onesie or hugging a penguin plushie. The name stuck partly because she looks a little bit like one and occasionally flaps her arms, but mainly because she walks like a penguin, with her feet awkwardly splayed outwards – no doubt a result of all that ballet. However, Mina is nothing if not a consummate idol. When the need arises – a red carpet or a stage runway – her walk is as refined as her dancing, even in high heels and tight dresses. Korean fans have dubbed this her 'capitalism walk' – put on when the Twice business requires it.

On rest days Mina is notorious for staying in bed as long as possible – often watching movies all day. As Twice's great introvert her hobbies are largely solitary, too. She loves Lego (and has displayed completed *Stranger Things* and *Harry Potter* sets) and will happily sit down in breaks in the schedule to knit, including beanies for the Save the Children charity. Her favourite pastime, though, is gaming. She's a big fan of *Elsword* (and has modelled for the game) and has posted a 20-minute video of her *Minecraft* game. In 2020 she revealed she had recently bought a gaming PC and accessories as she is now playing properly!

JYP wrote the lyrics for the 2019 single 'Feel Special' after having conversations with each of the members. Mina's verse talks of the world losing meaning and wanting to hide but being reassured by Once and by Twice. By the time the single was released in September, those words had taken on additional significance as it was announced that Mina was taking a break from Twice activities after being diagnosed with anxiety.

It was immensely brave of Mina to publicise her condition and JYP's action was a huge step forward for K-pop, an industry where mental health issues have long been swept under the carpet. As the world tour continued, both the group and Once ensured Mina was not forgotten. Twice left a space in their line when bowing, included a penguin plushie in group photos and told audiences that they would return as a nine-member group. Meanwhile, Once took the song 'After Moon' as their cue to honour Mina with chants and create a moving mint-green ocean with their lightsticks.

After appearing in some promotional activities in 2020, Mina made limited and low-key appearances on stage during the *Twicelights* Japanese tour. Then, on 11 February 2020, in Fukuoka, Mina joined the rest of the group to perform 'Feel Special' for the first time as a nine-member group and also spoke directly to the audience. The emotion of her fellow members and Once at seeing her bright, healthy and dancing as well as ever was immense. #ProudOfYouMina was soon trending worldwide. Their precious penguin had returned; they had worried about her, sorely missed her and were overjoyed to see her back on stage.

21

DAHYUN

Stage name: Dahyun (pronounced Ta-ion)
Birth name: Kim Da-hyun
Nicknames: Dubu, Dub-jussi
Lovely name: Davely
Twice colour: White
Nationality: Korean
Position: Lead rapper, sub-vocalist
Date of birth: 28 May 1998
Zodiac sign: Gemini
Blood type: O
Height: 159cm (5ft 3in)

'Dayhun is lacking in her rapping, singing and dancing.' It wasn't the greatest endorsement from JYP as he picked her as a member of Twice at the culmination of the *Sixteen* series. Fortunately, there was a caveat: 'The reason why I choose you,' he continued, 'is because you really grab the audience's attention.' The next five years would show that if the boss had underestimated Dahyun's performing skills, he had pinpointed her rare talent.

Dubu, as Once call her, is Twice's positive spirit. So extra and so funny, her personality adds yet another dimension to this multi-faceted group.

Dahyun was already something of a star before she joined JYP. She grew up in the city of Seongnam, a satellite city 20 kilometres to the southeast of Seoul. Along with her parents and her older brother, Myung Soo, she attended a Christian church and would often perform there. In 2011, when she was just 13 years old, a video of her dancing in church went viral. She looked super-confident as she performed an impressive dance, but what drove the views were the eye-opening moves in which she flapped her arms and whipped her hair back and forth. She became known as the Eagle Dance Church Sister and the dance was even adopted as an emote (character action) in the video game *Fortnite*.

This in itself might have alerted K-pop companies to Dayhun's extraordinary talents, but she was actually scouted the following year at a youth dance festival. Again, she stood out. She was a middle-school student among high-school and college competitors, and while they performed cover dances in dance crews, she took to the stage alone and danced to her own choreography. All the big three K-pop companies – JYP, SM and YG – invited her to audition and after getting offers from each of them, she chose JYP, because they had been the first to get in touch with her.

Dahyun joined JYP as a 14-year-old on 7 July 2012 and spent over three years as a trainee. It was hard work as each day she would start training as soon as she finished school. JYP knew she had confidence, but they discovered she had attitude, too. 'When I was told, "Do this, do that," while I was a trainee,' she said on the TV show *Same Bed, Different Dreams*, 'that made me not want to do it even more.' Jeongyeon has also spoken of how Dahyun was a chubby (if cute) child and was suspended as a trainee several times for not losing weight. Nevertheless, she earned a cameo as an initially cold-hearted schoolgirl in Got7's 2014 hit 'Stop Stop' and was on screen long enough to make a mark with her visuals and acting skills.

Dahyun carried her spirit and personality into the *Sixteen* competition. From the opening of her teaser when she misunderstood the director's instructions to clap for the camera, she won thousands of hearts and many more fell for her when the first mission saw her produce a dance that was not only full of charm, but also featured the famous eagle dance. Although her vocals and raps sometimes let her down, Dahyun's energy levels remained sky high and she was a firm favourite with the online voters.

Only one incident really threatened Dahyun's place in Twice. With her team, which included Tzuyu, Sana and Minyoung, struggling, Dahyun missed team practice on consecutive days. As the senior member, Sana took her to task and questioned her commitment. Dahyun tearfully apologised and the two made it up, with Sana's angry line, 'Did you think I was joking? I'm being totally serious' even becoming a running joke between them.

Still only 17 years old, Dahyun took her place as the third-youngest in the group and part of the *maknae* line. Her role in the group was as a rapper and with her soft-voiced style and smooth flow she provided a contrast to the group's other rapper, Chaeyoung. Of the two, it was Dahyun who first captured fans' attention. In 'TT' her cute expression when exclaiming '*Neomuhae!*' was enough to send it viral, then in 'Likey' her '*Jamkkanman jamkkanman*' rap line accompanied by a dab dance move (three years after it was a global craze) was an instant iconic moment.

In her *Sixteen* teaser, Dahyun revealed that she is known to her friends as Dubu, the Korean word for tofu, because her skin tone is so pale. In South Korea, porcelain skin colour is the basic standard of beauty which, combined with her monolid (an eye lid shape without a crease – also considered super-pretty) and cute personality, ensured she was a popular member of the group in her home nation. Once soon adopted the nickname, too, with international fans often calling her Tofu and sometimes adding an adjective, to make her Energetic Tofu or Flexible Tofu.

Of all the Twice members, it is Dahyun who has generated the most excitement over her changes of hair colour. She switched the pink and orange ombre from debut to blue and blonde for 'Cheer Up' and never stopped. She has been through ginger-orange ('TT'), dark brown ('Likey'), summer blonde ('Dance the Night Away'), a purple-blue ombre ('Yes or Yes'), denim-blue ('Fancy'), dark blue ('More and More') and several shades of brown. Each change is a careful secret, except … In April 2020, having worn a tightly tied hoodie to hide her new colour in public, Dahyun absent-mindedly joined Sana on V LIVE, only to realise after a few seconds that her new blue tresses were in full view. Her face was a picture!

Once soon got wise to another Dahyun trait: camera spotting. She claims she has a sixth sense for realising when she is being filmed from afar and immediately poses for it. She was certainly the only member who spotted the camera in the prank in the *Elegant Private Life* series, when she was in the lift with the kissing couple. YouTube compilations feature her in the midst of crowds looking straight at the camera, even when it's immediately overhead during busy fan signings. Needless to say, she is a champion photobomber – especially when MCs are presenting to camera!

Not that Dahyun is short on screen time. In variety shows, *Twice TV* and V LIVE broadcasts, she is among the loudest of the group, willing to be cheeky and make fun of herself. She delighted the crowd at a baseball match by joining in the ceremonial sliding; she brought the hosts of *Knowing Bros* to helpless laughter when she entered Momo and Mina's contemporary versus ballet competition with her own crazy style of dance; on *Running Man* she took on Momo in a dance competition with her own wacky moves; and on *Weekly Idol*, when she was asked to show her girl-crush vibes, she displayed great comic timing in her dance response (and destroyed the effect by saying 'wild and edgy' in the cutest English).

She is up for anything. In fact, she was so good on *Weekly Idol* that they invited her to be a guest host on several episodes; she was an MC at the Idol Star Athletics Championships; and also showed her acting skills playing opposite Astro's Cha Eun Woo in *Replies That Make Us Flutter*, a show that derived its plotline from viewers' comments. In a more serious mood, she also took part in the female edition of *Real Men*, where celebrities train and live the army life alongside real soldiers.

One particular appearance on *Knowing Bros* in 2019 received a lot of attention. Dahyun appeared opposite JYP and called her boss an idiot. The pair were playing charades when she jibed that he didn't know the rules of the game, ignoring the respectful language used to elders in Korean society. The encounter delighted K-pop fans who loved their idol's cheekiness.

In the Twice dorm, though, Dahyun is said to be a much quieter person. She's happy to spend time reading or playing piano and members have commented that she sometimes slopes off to bed when the rest are staying up to party. Off-duty and lounging around at home, she also wears loose, comfortable men's clothes, earning her the nickname Dub-jussi – a combination of Dubu and the Korean word for a middle-aged man. She originally shared a room with the other youngsters,

Chaeyoung and Tzuyu, and as they were the only ones still attending high school, the trio took the name School Lunch Club, with Dahyun as the leader. Together they had their own shows on V LIVE – *School Lunch Club Adventures* and *School Lunch Club Special Class* – which were always amusing, as Dahyun helped bring out the fun sides of the other two. Although Dahyun graduated from high school in February 2017, the School Lunch Club lives on.

There is also Saida, referred to constantly on fan forums. Ever since their argument on *Sixteen* Sana and Dahyun have been close friends. Once initially named the friendship Sada, but clever souls among them changed it to Siada – the Korean word for 'cider', which is actually a lemonade-type drink – to reflect their refreshing effect. When Dahyun injured her ankle, Sana reportedly accompanied her to hospital still wearing her slippers – although it says a lot for the closeness of the members that Jihyo carried her piggyback-style and Nayeon followed along in floods of tears. Of course, a social butterfly like Dahyun has made plenty of idol friendships outside the group, too. Among them are Dreamcatcher's Gahyeon, Sinb and Yerin from GFriend and Irene from Red Velvet. Among the male idols, she has been friends with Got7's Bambam since they were trainees together and has known Jooheon from Monsta X since her young teen days at church.

Dahyun would say she also has thousands of friends in Once. Many of them believe she gives the best fan service (a K-pop term for paying attention to fans). From visiting fanzones at concerts, to trying to reach fans who were behind a glass partition when she was an MC at the Idol Games to posting a (beautifully neat) handwritten letter of thanks on her 20th birthday. She also brings freshness and surprises to Twice's live shows. She is always engaging with the crowd, who especially love it when she lip syncs the translator, as if she is speaking Thai, Malaysian or English. The love she receives in return from the audience often reduces her to tears – but some Once have pointed out that even then she has the cutest habit of emerging from her tears with the brightest smile.

Those singing, rapping and dancing skills disparaged by JYP on *Sixteen* have improved immensely since Twice debuted. Since 2018, Dahyun has had more of an opportunity to show off her rapping skills. This culminated with 2019's 'Feel Special' – it was her best rap verse yet and included a staccato earworm of 'You make every-thing al-right'. Her dancing, too, was on point, especially in the live sub-unit special stages. She has shown she can do super-cute, as in the cover of Turbo's 'The Black Cat Nero', in which she and Tzuyu performed in catsuits, or super-sexy, as in the cover of Beyoncé's 'Dance for You', which she did with Sana and Tzuyu. On the *Twiceland* tour she revealed her first solo stage. Dressed in a three-piece suit (she discarded the jacket mid-song) and shades, she mesmerised audiences with her cool dance cover of Rain's classic 'Rainism', renaming it 'Dahyunism' and adding a perfectly executed cane dance in the break.

Dahyun's contributions to the group extends to helping choreograph 'Touchdown' and 'Jelly Jelly' and co-writing the rap parts of 'Missing U' and the lyrics to 'Trick It'. On stage and in videos Dahyun has also shown she plays the piano exquisitely, even impressing her fellow members. In 2019 an official Twice video on YouTube featured her playing a solo piano cover of South Korean pianist Yiruma's 'Reminiscent'. A year later, on her birthday, Dahyun uploaded another video, this time of her playing the piano and singing 'Feel Special'. It was beautiful and was viewed well over three million times in the first month. Those harsh words from JYP on *Sixteen* had never seemed so unwarranted. In her time with Twice, Dahyun has grown from a girl to a woman and her skills have developed to make her the perfect all-round idol.

22

CHAEYOUNG

Stage name: Chaeyoung (pronounced
   Chay-yong)
Birth name: Son Chae-young
Nicknames: Baby Beast, Baby Simba,
   Strawberry Princess, Chaeng,
   Chaengcasso
Lovely name: Chaengvely
Twice colour: Red
Nationality: Korean
Position: Main rapper, vocalist
Date of birth: 23 April 1999
Zodiac sign: Taurus
Blood type: B
Height: 159cm (5ft 3in)

As the smallest and second-youngest member of Twice, Chaeyoung sure packs a punch. With her cute voice and distinctive looks, there is no missing her in the group line-up, but there is so much more to this rapper than her stage persona. Chaeyoung is not a typical idol – she has a lively mind and is not afraid to express herself.

Chaeyoung grew up in the Dunchon Dong district in the heart of Seoul. Pictures of her as a child reveal the same well-proportioned facial features, beauty spot and large eyes that give her such an individual look (Nayeon thought she wasn't Korean when they first met!), while photos of her mother and her younger brother Jeong Hun show that good looks are a feature of the family.

She has described herself as a lively child and was a natural performer. She took acting classes at a young age, was a model for a children's magazine and briefly attended ballet lessons. In primary school she began to focus more on being a singer and at 13 started dance classes. She entered talent contests, often dancing to JYP group 2PM songs, and soon auditioned for Pledis Entertainment (home to boy band Nu'Est and girl group After School) and JYP, where she sang to 2NE1's 'It Hurts'. After two auditions she was accepted by JYP, much to her mother's delight as she was already a fan of the company.

Still only 13, Chaeyoung began life as a JYP trainee on 6 June 2012, a month before Dahyun and five months before Tzuyu. In a trainee project a few months later she discovered she had an aptitude for rap and began to focus on building her skills. She found dance a little more difficult, eventually passing the JYP basic routine dance exam after two and a half years (it took Momo three months!). The rumour mill suggests that as a trainee she had boyfriends (possibly Tao, formerly of EXO, and actor Kim Woo-bin), but, even if true, JYP rules soon put an end to that.

Alongside other future Twice members, Chaeyoung made brief appearances in videos for Got7's 'Stop Stop It' and Miss A's 'Only You', but her break came in 2015 when, after three years of training, JYP named her among the *Sixteen* hopefuls. Only just 16, many thought she was there to gain experience and would feature in the girl group JYP was planning for 2017, but Chaeyoung had other ideas. After all, Twice would need a rapper and she was one of the few contenders with that speciality.

In her teaser Chaeyoung set out her stall with a fierce rendition of Nicki Minaj's 'Stupid Hoe', kitted out in a silver one-piece and fluffy black jacket. In the first challenge, she justified her position in the major team with an awesome opening rap, and in the photoshoot round wore a pinstripe suit complete with cane and fake moustache for a cheeky but cute solo pic. Despite slaying JYP's own 'Honey' – to which she added a self-penned rap – Chaeyoung was relegated to the minors after losing to an inspired Jihyo. She then struggled to assert herself in the early team challenges and even seemed to be on the brink of elimination, only for Momo to exit the competition instead. Somehow, though, as the series entered its final stages, she managed to find her confidence and the craziness JYP was looking for.

On the eve of the final, she uttered the immortal line, 'The only way [to go] is to debut and become the best in the world … right?' The next day she took the first step by smashing her rap in the final performance. She had improved her singing, dancing and rapping throughout the competition, and won over both JYP and the voting audience to be named a member of Twice. She was thrilled, especially for her grandmother, who spent a lot of time looking after her (the other trainees loved the tuna *kimbap* that Chaeyoung brought back after visiting her), but was sad to see Somi, one of her best friends, fail to make the group.

Chaeyoung shares the role of lead rapper with Dahyun. Sometimes she's limited by splitting the short rap parts or by the cute nature of the songs, but her lines flow and she can rap fast or sweetly. Given the opportunity she can also spit bars. These usually come in cover performances, such as when she joined Jihyo, Nayeon and Tzuyu to perform 'Daring Women' on the show *Sugarman*; in Twice's cover of Wonder Girls' 'So Hot'; or when she earned the nickname Chaerianna Grande after the special stage performance of 'Greedy'. In the JYP stage at the 2018 KBS Song Festival she was the only female rapper, holding her own against Day6's Dowoon, Jae and Young K, Got7's BamBam, and Stray Kids' Han and Changbin.

She is also adept at writing rap parts for herself at live shows and cover performances, with perhaps the best being her feisty diatribe against Twice haters in a cover of Rhianna's 'Work' in the JYP Nation show just a year after the group's debut. She was also the first of the group to contribute to Twice's own songs. She wrote both her and Dahyun's rap in 'Precious Love' back in 2016 and has co-written lyrics for songs every year since, including favourites such as 'Missing U', 'Sweet Talker' (with Jeongyeon), 'Strawberry' and 'Sweet Summer Day'.

Throughout her training as a rapper at JYP, Chaeyoung kept singing, but once Twice debuted as a nine-member group, lines were always going to be hard to come by. She got to open 'Touchdown' and 'Feel Special', but often you have to look to the B-sides, such as 'Tuk Tok', 'You're in My Heart' and 'Missing You' to see her talent as a singer. She did appear more prominently on the *More and More* EP, singing the hook on the title track and featuring on 'Oxygen' and 'Shadow', perhaps indicating she will find more opportunities in the future. At the moment, though, the best example of her sweet vocal style is probably her 2016 Melody Project in which she sung a hauntingly beautiful version of Cheeze's ballad 'Alone'.

Twice members themselves have voted Chaeyoung as the most talented member of the group, referring not only to her performance skills but her artistic nature, too. She likes to make films, take photos, write poetry, paint and draw. On variety shows she has produced very accurate caricatures of the others and her drawings have been used on album-cover artwork, a face mask, tote bag and limited-edition Spris trainers. She has a Picasso quote – 'Painting is just another way of keeping a diary' – on her bedroom wall and is a massive fan of artists Basquiat and Hundertwasser. No wonder fans sometimes refer to her as Chaengcasso!

It is sometimes easy to forget that Chaeyoung is just a month older than Tzuyu. They were in the same class at high school, graduating together in February 2019. Dahyun was in the year above and leads their School Lunch Club V LIVE broadcasts and adventures. Not that she is limited to one gang – she also links up with Jeongyeon, when the pair are known as the No Jam Brothers for their slightly strange shared sense of humour. She is also close to Nayeon (a friendship that Once call Nachaeng), who she says knows most about her, and Mina (Michaeng) – Once love this pairing as they are so sweet to each other.

On one occasion, in a conversation in the dorm, Chaeyoung revealed her parents call her Strawberry Princess due to her love of strawberries. Naturally, every kind of strawberry accessory was soon being sent her way by Chaeyoung fans. Once, though, came up with their own nickname. They call her Baby Beast, because they think her big eyes and slightly pointed teeth make her look like a baby lion or a tiger cub. She plays along by wearing lion onesies, cuddling lion plushies and was even invited to the 2019 premiere of the *Lion King* movie as K-pop's own 'Baby Simba'.

These nicknames celebrated Chaeyoung's role as Twice's own 'smol bean' – petite but precious and so cute you want to keep her in your pocket. Which is true-ish. However, Chaeyoung can also look athletic, chic and, as she has grown older, seductive and sexy. She is something of a chameleon: teasing in her school uniform and long dark hair; totally cute with bangs and pigtails; a princess as the yellow ballerina of 'What is Love?'; making a statement with short pink hair in the 'Fancy' era; and she can still pull off space buns with an elegant flared-sleeve dress in 'More & More'.

Having watched her hair go from red to orange to mint to platinum blonde (the long, straight orange was most popular, but she prefers black), more recently Chaeyoung watchers have discovered a new hobby – tattoo-spotting. During the *Twicelights* tour in June 2019, Chaeyoung appeared with a strawberry lips tattoo on her wrist. As the summer progressed, a cherry tomato was spotted on her shoulder. The game was on and soon pictures revealed four tiny carrots on her forearm and, best of all, a tattoo tribute to Twice's 'Shot Thru the Heart' track on her neck. Next came a fish, just above her elbow, that Chaeyoung had designed herself. Once remain alert for any additions.

Among K-pop idols, especially female idols, having a tattoo is still a brave move. Korean society is very conservative and until recently has frowned upon this type of body art. It is typical of Chaeyoung that she broke the taboo. In an interview with *Marie Claire* magazine in 2019, Jeongyeon said how much she admired Chaeyoung's 'decisive and free nature' – she doesn't think too deeply and does what she wants to do. A further example of this was when she cut her hair after falling in love with actress Kristen Stewart's short hairstyle. She hadn't even told the company and said JYP was taken aback when he saw her, asking if she would at least let them know if she was going to do anything like that again.

Kristen Stewart emerged as Chaeyoung's role model again in a 2019 interview with *GQ Korea* magazine, when she referred to the actress wearing Converse shoes with her dress at the Cannes Film Festival. 'I also want to become someone who breaks the unspoken rules,' Chaeyoung said. 'Some people think of idols as just pretty and cute people with lots of *aegyo*, but I want to expand that image.'

With her artistic interests and a taste in music that includes underground and obscure Korean and Western artists, Chaeyoung is increasingly seen as Twice's free spirit. She refuses to hide behind a mask when out alone in public, prefers to wear vintage clothes rather than designer outfits, and took to the group's Instagram to call out a stalker who had targeted both her and Nayeon. She seems eager to break down the mystique surrounding idols: she asked to show her face when Nayeon was on a V LIVE to prove that idols have bad skin days just like everyone else and has said how she resists the urge to lose weight by trying to accept how she is.

Chaeyoung has also been at the centre of Twice's evolution into a modern K-pop group who are willing to speak out about mental-health issues. She has encouraged fans to have faith in themselves and not to compare themselves to others, and she has also stressed the importance of being aware of one's mental well-being and of positivity. 'I want to become an artist who can readily create and express myself,' she told *Allure Korea*. 'I want to be someone who can inspire and help others.' She might still be as small as when she debuted, but since then Twice's Baby Beast has grown in so many ways.

23

TZUYU

Stage name: Tzuyu (pronounced
    Choo-wee)
Birth name: Chou Tzu-yu
Nicknames: Chewy, Yoda, Freedom
Lovely name: Tzuvely
Twice colour: Blue
Nationality: Taiwanese
Position: Lead dancer, vocalist, *maknae*
Date of birth: 14 June 1999
Zodiac sign: Gemini
Blood type: A
Height: 172cm (5ft 8in)

Since 1990, the US film review site TC Candler has been ranking the world's most beautiful women. Past winners have
included supermodels such as Jourdan Dunn and actresses Emma
Watson and Keira Knightley, but in 2019 they named Twice's
youngest member, Tzuyu, as having the most beautiful face in
the world. It wasn't news to K-pop fans. They'd been aware of

her superlative beauty even since she appeared as a shy 15-year-old in the *Sixteen* series.

As soon as her teaser for *Sixteen* was released tongues started wagging about this tall, exotic-looking contestant with the cutest face and a perfectly proportioned body. By the end of the first episode, a gif of her had gone viral on Korean K-pop sites. They were captivated by this girl who didn't conform to Korean standards of beauty, didn't look like other foreign K-pop stars, but was stunningly attractive.

Despite the initial response, few gave this Taiwanese trainee a chance. Visuals counted for a lot, but not everything. Tzuyu was awkward and showed no great talent for singing or dancing. But then something amazing happened. As the series progressed, the viewers fell in love with her and as she gained confidence she blossomed. She began to reveal her talent in the one-on-one challenge against the super-popular Nayeon. Tzuyu performed the Pussycat Dolls' 'Sway' and, although it wasn't faultless, it showed she could go head to head with a proven singer. 'She's so pretty,' said her worried opponent, 'that I can't even notice her mistakes.' Tzuyu went to the top of the online rankings, although as yet JYP remained unconvinced of the youngster's potential.

When Tzuyu teamed up with Jeongyeon and Nayeon, it was a game-changer. They helped transform her from pretty to alluring and she was inspired by the older trainees to take her singing and dancing to another level. Performing Miss A's 'Hush' with them seemed to open JYP's eyes to the talents of the girl who celebrated her 16th birthday in the middle of the series. He was further impressed with how she won the hearts of all her rivals on the show and, in the series finale, concluded that maybe the audience knew something after all. He congratulated her as the trainee whose skills had most improved and explained how this showed him that she had the passion to succeed. In a move that shocked and delighted the viewers, he added Tzuyu to the Twice line-up. It was a decision he would never regret.

Tzuyu was set to be the first major K-pop star to hail from Taiwan, which was surprising given the country has a massive interest in Korean music. Taiwan already took national pride in the success of Amber Liu from the girl group f(x), but, although both her parents were from Taiwan, she was born and raised in the USA. Tzuyu was the real deal. Born in Tainan City, Taiwan, Tzuyu was the daughter of night-market traders. She loved singing and dancing and attended classes from a young age. In 2012 her dance performance at Tainan's MUSE Performing Art Workshop was uploaded online. Tzuyu's tall and agile figure stood out enough to be spotted by JYP Entertainment scouts, who invited her to South Korea for auditions. By November 2012 she had transferred to a middle school in Seoul and begun life as a trainee.

By the time she took part in *Sixteen* Tzuyu had been a trainee for two and a half years. In that period she didn't spend much time with the other future members of Twice. Of course they knew of her. According to Nayeon, her beauty was legendary, even before she arrived at the company, and her looks got her noticed at internal JYP showcases. Tzuyu, however, spoke no Korean when she began at JYP and that made it difficult for her to connect with other trainees. Even when she was on *Sixteen*, her Korean was far from fluent.

When the Twice line-up was finally selected, Tzuyu was named as the *maknae* – the youngest member – of the group. This is a special position in any K-pop group and it has many privileges and few obligations. The *maknae* doesn't have to feature heavily in recordings and performances and is allowed to be shy and quiet on variety shows. This suited Tzuyu very well. She was only just 16, was an introvert by nature and still lacked confidence when speaking Korean. Fortunately, she had older members who were happy to look after her. She shared a room with her soon-to-be School Lunch Club friends, Dahyun and Chaeyoung, but Jihyo was especially attentive and before Tzuyu moved into the dorm Jeongyeon had already put all her belongings away for her.

Initially Tzuyu's impact was visual. She was easily the tallest of the Twice members and was not difficult to pick out, with her shiny long hair and distinctive darker skin tone. Her outfits emphasised her long legs, curvy hips and tiny waist, and even her fellow members marvelled at her slender figure. She immediately featured as one of the most popular members in polls in Korea and overseas, and soon after debut appeared in an advert for LG, in which she danced seductively in a lift. On variety shows she didn't say a lot, adeptly flipping her tongue or twitching her ears when called upon to perform her party piece, but her coyness just added to her charm.

Tzuyu had a further reason to be reticent. Just months after debuting she had inadvertently sparked a national incident by holding aloft the flag of the Republic of China – a symbol of Taiwanese independence – on a Korean variety show. The reaction in mainland China led to a boycott of JYP Entertainment acts and Huawei, a Chinese company, cancelled their endorsement deal with Tzuyu. Looking nervous and upset, Tzuyu then uploaded an apology video. It was a tough ordeal for one so young to deal with and, for a while, she seemed to lose what little confidence she had built up.

What she did exhibit was a certain inner strength and it was a characteristic her fellow members noticed. Whereas most of them were often overcome with emotion, Tzuyu rarely cried in public. Her tears first appeared in June 2016 when she was a guest on a food show called *Please Take Care of My Refrigerator*. As she tucked into some delicious Chinese wraps, her fellow guest Jeongyeon explained that they reminded Tzuyu of her mum – which was enough to make the poor girl burst into tears. However, she still had a reputation for being reserved until one day Jihyo explained that Tzuyu actually cries more often than any of the girls, sometimes out of the blue, and has a really gentle heart.

The members, of course, look after their *maknae*, whose name sounds like the Korean word for freedom, which is why that's one of her nicknames. Jihyo and Jeongyeon came up with a better one, though, as they think her big eyes and pointy ears make her look like a cute version of Yoda. When Tzuyu turned up to dance practice in a *Star Wars* t-shirt, the name stuck and she regularly brings Yoda toys and lightsabers to fan meetings. It was also at a fan meeting in 2016 that Tzuyu was asked what she would like for her birthday. She meant to say she wanted love from all the members, but when she mistakenly said kisses instead, she began a group tradition of giving members special kisses on their birthday.

Her language mishaps can be very amusing. In Twice's first year she appeared on a show where she spent the day with Got7's Jackson and others. When asked about her trip at the end of the show, Tzuyu replied, 'Today was really boring ...' To be fair, the words for fun and boring are very similar in Korean. On other occasions she can be incredibly cute. That includes the time she was playing a game where she had to say a word beginning with the last syllable of the previous answer. With limited vocabulary, Tzuyu delivered the words '*Mommy saranghae*' – 'I love you, Mummy'. Random and totally sweet, it became one of Once's favourite gifs.

Once know that Tzuyu can be savage as well as cute. She gives straightforward responses that come out as hilarious. When the cast of *Knowing Bros* asked who she wanted to sit next to, she scanned the show's hosts carefully before replying, 'I don't really care.' Or when Nayeon offered to drive her around once she got her driving licence, Tzuyu responded, 'I'll go in Jihyo's car.' Once's favourite Tzuyu retorts include the time backstage at the MAMAs when Jihyo lovingly told Tzuyu, who wasn't feeling well, that she was her medicine and, without a pause, received the reply, 'That's why I haven't been cured yet!' And, at the aquarium, when Jihyo (again) wondered if she fell in and was attacked by sharks whether Tzuyu would save her and Tzuyu deadpanned, 'I don't know how to swim.'

As much as they might have wanted to, Once couldn't keep Tzuyu to themselves. She was just too beautiful. Again and again images of her would go viral, bringing in new fans from around the world. As fabulous as she looked on stage and in video, these photos were often taken when she was off guard. At the 2016 Idol Games she was snapped as she took her shot in the archery competition and an arrowhead flicked her hair. It was so graceful it caught everyone's attention – even Hollywood film directors. Then there was the shot of her in bat deely-boppers that was reposted endlessly across Japan or the 2020 snap of her dressed down in a simple white t-shirt, without make-up, her hair tied up, that went viral.

When Twice debuted Tzuyu went on record as saying she wanted to be more than just a visual in the group and, despite having to sing in Korean, Japanese and English, all foreign languages for her, she has proved that she is a dependable and versatile vocalist. She can adjust her range and tone from song to song, with her parts on 'Precious Love' and 'Rollin'', and a chorus in 'Signal' highlighting her talent. Her singing has become more confident and on tracks like 'Brand New Girl' she has had enough lines to make a real impression. Similarly, her dancing

— always smooth and elegant — has become more assured. As she has matured, she has also been able to perform more sensuous moves, as exhibited in the Beyoncé cover dances in Twice live shows. This culminated in a killer performance at SBS's *Gayo Daejeon* in December 2019, when she took part in a mirrored dance alongside AOA's Seolhyun to 'Do You' by TroyBoi.

As she has grown up in the spotlight, more facets of Tzuyu have emerged. She is friends with other idols, including CLC's Elkie and fellow Taiwanese Shuhua from (G)I-dle. She is sporty: she learned to ride a skateboard for an ad (inspiring a fan to create a Tzuyu Skate Twice mobile game) and excelled at archery at the Idol Games. She loves dogs: she dotes on her own incredibly sweet Pomeranian, Gucci, but she has also volunteered at dog rescue centres. She also showed her creative side when she designed a rubbish bin for their *Twicelights* world tour. Featuring the phrase, 'Throw your negative energy here', the bold design continued to sell out every time it was restocked. Her cookery skills, however, have been found wanting. The members confirm she is the worst cook in Twice and her two-hour V LIVE cookery broadcast in 2017 was a culinary disaster — but still amassed a billion views!

Tzuyu turned 21 in 2020. She is the pride of Taiwan (following the 'flag incident', even older Taiwanese are fans) and an all-round performer in Twice. Once have watched her not only grow in stature on stage but also seen her develop into an articulate young adult. She may be the most beautiful woman in the world but, more importantly, she is an integral member of Twice.

PICTURE CREDITS

Page 6
Top © Imaginechina Limited/Alamy Stock Photo
Bottom © THE FACT/Imazins via Getty Images

Pages 7 and 8
© The Chosunilbo JNS/Imazins via Getty Images

INDEX

aegyo (use of cute voices, facial expressions and gestures) 3, 20, 38, 56, 79, 82, 87, 90, 100, 108, 109, 160, 168, 176, 179, 187, 192, 193, 200, 206, 227
'After Moon' 128, 141, 177, 211
Aitken, Hayley 147
Akihito, Emperor 139–40, 194
Alexander, Sean 109
'all-kill' (topping all daily and real-time charts) 61, 64, 80, 92, 97
Amber, David 109, 126
&Twice 153–4, 156
AOA 42, 50, 109, 155, 235
Apink 32, 50, 53
Astro 71, 217
award shows 5 *see also individual award show name*

Baby V.O.X. 49
Baek Ji Young 116
BDZ (album) 125, 134

'BDZ' (single) 124–5, 126, 128, 133
'Be As One' 125, 126, 132, 209
Beat to the End 53
Beautiful Twice 74
Bestie 53
'bias' (favourite member of a group) 39, 67, 84, 97, 186, 208
'bias-wreckers' (members who make fans question their original choice) 39
Big Bang 6, 47, 98, 138, 143
Big Hit Entertainment 2
Billboard charts 12, 29, 37, 68, 80, 92, 97, 100, 102, 104, 105, 115, 121, 126, 128, 143, 144, 161, 170
Black Eyed Pilseung 32, 61, 78, 90, 103, 135
Blackpink 6, 7, 46, 73, 82, 84, 136, 143, 169
BoA 143
'Brand New Girl' 112, 234

'Breakthrough' 140, 148, 153
BTS 2, 6, 46, 53, 64, 71, 72, 85, 91, 92, 99, 100, 110, 132, 137, 138, 143, 169

'C' 44
Cabello, Camila 111
Candy Bong (lightstick) 75–6, 134, 138
Candy Bong Z (lightstick) 138, 144
'Candy Boy' 37, 51, 75–6
'Candy Pop' 111, 112, 134, 209
Carefree Traveller 108
Carpenter, Sabrina 111
Cecilia 13–14
'centre' (most prominent member in group photographs/ choreography) 79, 167
CGV 51
Chaeryeong 16, 18, 20, 21, 22, 132
Chaeyeon 16, 17, 21, 22, 182
Chaeyoung 50, 73, 98, 100, 102, 103, 107, 114, 116, 132, 133, 135, 139, 141, 144, 150, 154–5, 158, 169, 171, 182, 191, 215, 218, 221–7; 'BDZ' and 124; 'Brand New Girl' and 112; 'Candy Pop' and 111; 'Cheer Up' and 61, 62; 'Dance the Night Away' and 121, 160; 'Eyes, Eyes, Eyes' and 97, 201; 'Fancy' and 136; 'Feel Special' and 147; first awards shows with Twice 48; first Christmas with Twice 49; 'How U Doin' and 154; 'Ice Cream' and 93; Idol Star Athletics Championships and 53; 'Jelly

Jelly' and 81; 'Knock Knock' and 91; 'Likey' and 110; 'Missing U' and 105; 'Next Page' and 82; No Jam Brothers (Chaeyoung and Jeongyeon) 42, 115, 177, 225; 'One More Time' and 101; PPAP craze and 76; 'Precious Love' and 67; *Signal* and 96, 97; 'Strawberry' and 137; 'Sweet Summer Day' and 160; 'Sweet Talker' and 178; 'TT' and 77, 79, 80; '21:29' and 149; Twice debut and 25, 26, 27, 33, 36, 38, 42, 43; *Twiceland – The Opening* and 87; Twice origins and background of 15–16, 17, 18, 19, 20, 222–4; *Twice's Elegant Private Life* and 59; USA/Europe, popularity in 86; 'Yes or Yes' and 127; 'Young and Wild' and 128
Charlie XCX 137
'Cheer Up' 60–4, 66, 68, 69, 70, 71, 73, 76, 83, 85, 87, 102, 103, 109, 111, 139, 170, 178, 183, 189, 191, 202, 208, 216
'Chillax' 122
China 1, 13, 14, 52, 85, 232, 233
Choi Kyu-sung 32
CLC 29, 47, 235
Collapsedone (Woo Min Lee) 90, 111, 113
colour pop 31, 32, 33, 37, 61
comebacks 6, 22, 60, 66, 75, 76, 77, 80, 86, 95, 102, 114, 120, 126, 127, 137, 158, 162, 179, 184, 195
Comedy Big League 74
cosplay 78, 99, 171
Covid-19 pandemic 157

cutesy (girl–next–door appeal) 4, 38, 63, 82, 84, 116, 124, 136, 145, 153, 179, 207, 217, 219, 230

Daedongjae season 69
Dahyun 49, 50, 53, 56, 57, 58, 59, 62, 67, 73, 76, 79, 80, 86, 87, 89, 91, 98, 100, 107, 108, 110, 113, 114, 115, 116, 120, 132, 135, 137, 139, 141, 145, 150, 155, 157, 158, 168, 191, 213–20, 222, 223, 224, 225, 232; 'BDZ' and 124; 'Cheer Up' and 70; 'Dahyunism' and 116, 219; 'Fancy' and 136; 'Feel Special' and 147, 219; 'Heart Shaker' and 109; 'Ice Cream' and 93; 'Jelly Jelly' and 81, 219; 'LaLaLa' and 128; 'Likey' and 103, 104; 'Missing U' and 105, 219; 'One More Time' and 101; 'Signal' and 96; 'Trick It' and 148, 219; '21:29' and 149; Twice debut 25, 26, 27, 31, 33, 36, 38, 39, 41, 42, 43; Twice origins and background of 15, 17, 18, 20, 21, 213–16; 'Yes or Yes' and 126, 127
'Dance the Night Away' 120–2, 134, 160, 168, 178, 179, 202, 216
Davichi 71
debuts 2; Twice 25–34
Defconn 41
'Dejavu' 115
Descendants of the Sun 59
DIA 29
'Do it Again' 20, 34, 37, 38, 60, 191
'Don't Call Me Again' 160

#Dreamday tour 133–5, 138, 139
Dream High 2 166

Elle 39, 40
Elsword 51, 210
entertainment companies 1–2 *see also individual company name*
Eunsuh 16, 18, 21, 22–3, 182
'Everyone's Doing the Nori' 76
EXID 53
EXO 6, 47, 50, 55, 85, 138, 222
'Eyes, Eyes, Eyes' 97

'Fake & True' 153
'Fancy' 135–7, 150, 179, 184, 195, 202, 208, 226
Fancy You 135–7, 143
fandoms 6; Twice 45–54 *see also individual fandom name*
Feel Special (EP) 146–50, 154, 160, 170, 201
'Feel Special' (single) 146–8, 153, 154, 155, 157, 171, 184, 194, 195, 210–11, 219, 224
'FFW' 105
Fin.K.L 6
'Firework' 160
5Live 13
4minute 32
Fromis_9 23
f(x) 4, 97, 231

Gag Concert 186
Galactika 109
Gaon Album Chart 37, 68
G–Dragon 64
generations, K–Pop 6–7
'Get Loud' 148, 201

GFriend 29, 47, 50, 57, 84, 122, 169, 202, 218
(G)I-dle 7, 235
'girl crush' 4, 33, 38, 40, 56, 82, 107, 116, 124, 135, 136, 139, 159, 173, 176, 179, 217
Girl's Day 53
Girls' Generation 4, 6, 12, 29, 50, 57, 65, 68, 71, 73, 83, 85, 86, 97, 98, 102, 143, 161, 166, 190, 206
'Girls Like Us' 137, 201
g.o.d 12, 31
God's Voice 74
Golden Disc Awards (GDAs) 5, 55–6, 86, 112, 134, 156, 206
Got7 13, 31, 32, 35, 48, 49, 50, 53, 73, 84, 166, 167, 169, 183, 190, 215, 218, 222, 224, 233
Grande, Ariana 17, 98, 155, 167, 170, 224

'Happy Happy' 140, 153
'Heart Shaker' 109–10, 115, 116, 126, 139, 170, 184
Heechul 70–1, 156, 186–7
'A History of K-pop with Twice' 50
'Ho!' 115, 201
'Hold Me Tight' 97
'Hot' 137
Hot Blood Men 15
'How U Doin' 154
Hyerim 73, 105
Hyuna 32
Hyungwon 72

'I'm Gonna Be a Star' 20, 68, 87, 170

'Ice Cream' 89, 93, 97, 103, 209
Idol Radio 185
Idol Room 126, 168
Idol School 23
Idol Star Athletics Championships (Idol Games) 53, 122, 132, 217, 218, 234, 235
iKon 50
Infinite 41
Inkigayo 29, 38, 57, 66, 68–9, 81, 82, 110, 114, 178, 209
Instagram 46, 71, 102, 139, 150, 187, 194, 227
I.O.I. 24, 67
Itzy 7, 22, 132–3, 134–5
'I Want You Back' 120, 125
Iz*One 7, 22, 202

Japan 22, 35, 44, 62, 81, 87, 114, 126; Twice members from 1, 2, 11, 14, 15, 19, 26, 52, 59, 60, 86, 100, 108, 122, 181, 182, 183, 185, 186, 189, 193, 205, 206; Twice success in 37, 59, 60, 80, 85, 92, 93, 98, 99–102, 104, 105, 110–12, 115, 117, 119, 120, 122, 123, 124–5, 128, 132, 133–5, 137, 138, 139, 140, 153, 154, 155, 156, 161, 234
Japanese Golden Disc Awards 134
'Jelly Jelly' 81, 219
Jeongyeon 49, 53, 56, 57, 58, 59, 61, 62, 70, 73, 76, 77, 79, 84, 86, 87, 89, 91, 96, 98, 107, 108, 109, 110, 121, 126, 136, 137, 139, 158, 159, 173–9, 185, 192, 200, 207, 214, 224, 225, 226, 230, 232, 233; 'Born this Way' and 154; 'Feel

Special and 146, 147; 'Firework' and 160; 'LaLaLa' and 128, 178; 'Likey' and 103, 104, 179; 'Love Line' and 105; 'My Ear's Candy' and 116; 'One More Time' and 101; *Signal* and 97; Twice debut and 25, 26, 27, 28, 30, 31, 32, 33, 36, 38, 39, 42, 43, 173–4; Twice origins and background of 13, 15, 17, 18, 19, 20, 21, 88, 166, 174–7; *Twicetagram* and 102, 103, 104, 105; 2Yeon (friendship Nayeon and Jeongyeon) 116, 169, 177; 'What is Love?' and 114, 115, 179; 'Yes or Yes' and 126–7

Jihyo 51, 56, 62, 66–7, 98, 100, 107, 108, 113, 114, 116, 123, 129, 139, 149, 155, 158, 178, 186, 191, 193, 197–203, 218, 223, 224, 232, 233, 234; 'A History of K-pop with Twice' and 50; 'BDZ' and 124; 'Dance the Night Away' and 121, 202; 'Eyes, Eyes, Eyes' and 97, 201; 'Feel Special' and 147; 'Get Loud' 148, 201; 'Girls Like Us' and 137, 201; 'Heart Shaker' and 109; 'Ho!' and 115; Kang Daniel and 145, 202; 'Knock Knock' and 92, 202; leader of Twice 18, 28, 48, 93, 107, 124, 177, 195, 199, 200, 201, 203; 'Likey' and 103, 169; 'One More Time' and 101; posts open letter to the Twice fans 156; 'Signal' and 96; 'Sunset' and 128, 201; 'TT' and 78, 79, 80, 81, 84, 99, 202; '24/7' and 105, 170, 201;

Twice debut and 25, 26, 27, 28, 30, 33, 38, 41, 43; Twice origins and background of 13, 15, 17, 18, 19, 20, 21, 88, 166, 175, 177, 191, 193, 197–200; *Twice's Elegant Private Life* and 58; *Twiceland* and 87, 88, 93; 'Yes or Yes' and 127

Jiwon 15, 17, 18, 19, 21, 23, 182

Jonghyun 141

Jung Eun Ji 66

Jungkook 64, 72

Jun.K 20, 184

Just Dance 2 167

JYP (Park Jin-young) 31, 48, 76, 91, 111, 122, 123, 131, 140–1, 144, 154, 155, 157, 167, 168, 169, 175, 211, 217; origins of Twice/*Sixteen* and 12–24, 25, 161, 181, 183, 190, 191, 199, 207, 213, 214, 219–20, 222, 223, 224, 226, 230, 231; Twice debut and 27, 29, 31, 32, 35, 44; Twice songwriting and 48, 61, 90, 95, 98, 103, 109, 113, 124, 126, 127, 146, 159, 182, 208, 210

JYP Entertainment 2; origins of Twice/*Sixteen* and 12–24, 166, 167, 169, 174, 175, 183, 190, 198, 202, 206, 207, 214, 222, 234, 231; Twice career, guidance of 46, 48, 50, 51, 52, 60, 61–2, 63, 64, 66, 68, 70, 72–3, 75, 76, 82, 86, 90, 91, 95, 98, 99, 103, 108, 109, 111, 113, 122, 123, 124, 126, 127, 131, 132, 138, 140, 141, 144, 145, 146, 148, 149, 154, 155, 157, 159, 161, 162, 184, 185, 1191, 192, 208, 209, 213, 217, 219, 224, 226, 230;

Twice debut and 25, 27, 28, 30, 31, 32, 34, 35, 44
JYP Nation 72–3, 108, 224

Kang Daniel 145, 202
Kara 98, 134, 190
KB Kookmin Bank 51, 76
KCON 59–60, 71, 98, 123, 144
K-drama 64
Kiel Tutin 136, 149
Kim Min-kyo 59
King of Mask Singer 56, 74, 201
'Knock Knock' 89–92, 93, 97, 170, 171, 202, 209
Knowing Bros 4, 70, 108, 126, 155, 156, 168, 186, 192, 209, 217, 234
Kōhaku (annual Japanese New Year's Eve TV special) 110–11
Korean Music Awards 5
Korean wave (*hallyu*) 6, 12, 26, 98, 100, 119, 190
K-Pop Star 15, 16
Kthe1 41

Lady Gaga 139, 144, 175
'LaLaLa' 128, 178
Larsson, Zara 159
leader, group 2, 28, 48, 93, 107, 121, 124, 168, 177, 197, 199, 200, 203, 208, 218
Lee Hyori 57, 182
Lena 13, 14
Let's Dance 41
Lewis, Sam 33, 61
Lia Kim 39, 185
lightsticks 75, 138, 141, 144, 145, 211
'Like a Fool' 33, 37, 194

'Like Ooh Ahh'. 31–3, 35, 37, 41, 43, 50, 51, 56, 60, 73, 83, 87, 99, 127, 162, 171, 184, 191, 208, 209
'Likey' 102, 103–4, 108–9, 110, 132, 135, 169–70, 179, 183, 195, 209, 215, 216
'lines' (sub-groups) 2, 100, 185, 215
'Look at Me' 105
'L.O.V.E' 125
'Love Foolish' 148
'Love Line' 105, 178
Love Live! School Idol Project 187
Lovelyz 29, 47, 50
Lucky Chouette 80
'Luv Me' 101–2

'Make Me' 160
'Make Me Go' 170
maknae (youngest member of group) 2, 25–6, 42, 57, 122, 123, 165, 168, 200, 215, 229, 231, 233
MAMA (Mnet Asian Music Awards) 5, 83, 108–9, 156
Mamamoo 29
MC Doni (Jung Hyung Don) 79
M Countdown 29, 37–8, 39, 51, 57, 63, 66–7, 68, 80, 114, 137–8, 202
Merry and Happy (album) 110
'Merry and Happy' (single) 110
Michaels, Julia 159
Mihawk Back 150
Mina 49, 50, 56, 58, 59, 73, 80, 82, 84, 86, 87, 91, 97, 102, 108, 110, 112, 114, 116, 137–8, 139, 158, 161, 177, 184, 191, 205–11, 217, 225; 'Candy Pop' and 111; 'Cheer Up' and 60, 62, 208, 209; 'Dance

the Night Away' and 122; 'Fancy' and 136; 'Feel Special' and 146, 147, 210–11; 'Likey' and 104, 209; 'Signal' and 96; struggles with extreme anxiety and insecurity 140–1, 144, 145, 146, 147, 149, 150, 151, 154, 155, 156, 157, 161, 193, 205, 211; 'TT' and 77, 78, 209; Twice debut 25, 26, 27, 33, 36, 38, 39, 40, 42, 208; Twice origins and background of 14, 15, 17, 18, 19, 20, 21, 206–8; 'What is Love?' and 113, 208; 'Yes or Yes' and 126, 127, 208

Minyoung 13, 15, 17, 18, 19, 20, 21, 23, 191, 215

Miss A 4, 12, 13, 14, 31, 32, 33, 35, 132, 166, 198

'Missing U' 105, 219, 224

MMA (Melon Music Awards) 5

MNEK 159

Mnet channel 5, 14, 37, 47, 83

Momo 48–9, 50, 53, 56, 58, 59, 62, 71, 73, 77, 86, 87, 91, 97, 104, 108, 109, 110, 112, 114, 116, 123, 133, 139, 144, 155, 157, 158, 170, 177, 181–8, 190, 191, 193, 207, 209, 217, 222, 223; 'Cheer Up' and 60, 183; 'Dance the Night Away' and 122; 'Fancy' and 184; 'Feel Special and 146, 147; 'Heart Shaker' and 184; Heechul, dates 156, 186–7; 'Hot' and 137; 'Likey' and 104, 183; 'Love Foolish' and 148; 'More & More' and 160; Peach Sisters (Nayeon and) 157, 169; 'Say You Love Me' and 128; 'Signal' and 96; 'TT' and 78–9,

81, 84; Twice debut and 25, 26, 27, 30, 34, 36, 38, 39, 40, 42, 43, 182–3; Twice origins and background of 14, 15, 17, 18–19, 21, 22, 131, 181–3; 'What is Love?' and 113, 184; 'Yes or Yes' and 127

Mone 14

Monsta X 50, 71, 72, 218

monster rookies 29

More & More (EP) 158–62

'More & More' (single) 159–60, 161, 162

MTV 66, 148, 149

M2 X Genie Music Awards (MGMA) 128–9

Muscle Queen Project 176

Music Bank 29, 38, 49, 51, 66, 68, 80, 83, 112, 114

Music Core 29, 38, 66, 161

music shows 4 *see also individual music show name*

Music Station 100, 111, 119

'Must Be Crazy' 20, 34

My Dream Class 178

'My Headphones On' 67, 178

My Little Television 52

Naïve Productions 35–6, 61–2

Nam, Eric 71

Naohiko Kyogoku 111

Natty 16, 17, 18, 20, 21, 23–4, 207

Nayeon 48, 49, 51, 53, 56, 57, 58, 59, 61, 70, 73, 76, 77, 80, 82, 84, 86, 87, 88, 89, 91, 96, 98, 107, 110, 112, 123, 124, 126, 131, 139, 150, 154, 155, 157, 158, 160, 165–72, 177, 178, 185, 193, 198,

200, 207, 218, 222, 224, 225, 227, 230, 231, 234; 'BDZ' and 133; 'Candy Pop' and 111; 'Cheer Up' and 62, 63, 170; 'Feel Special' and 147, 171; 'Heart Shaker' and 109, 170; 'I'm Gonna Be a Star' 68, 170; 'Ice Cream' and 93; 'Knock Knock' and 92, 170; 'Likey' and 103, 104, 169; 'Look at Me' and 105; 'Make Me' and 160; 'My Ear's Candy' and 116; 'One More Time' and 101; 'Rainbow' and 148; 'TT' and 78, 79; Twice debut and 25, 26, 27, 30, 33, 36, 40, 41, 42, 43; Twice origins and background 13, 15, 17, 18, 19, 20, 21, 165–7, 175; *Twicetagram* and 102, 170, 201; 'What is Love?' 113, 114; 'Yes or Yes' and 127

'Next Page' 81–2

No Jam Brothers 115, 177, 225

Oh My Girl 53, 177

Ollipop 147

Once (Twice fandom) 6, 55, 56, 57, 58, 59, 60, 61–2, 66, 67, 68, 69, 70, 73, 74, 76, 77, 78, 80, 81, 82, 83, 84, 85, 86–7, 88, 89, 92, 93, 94, 97, 98, 99, 100, 101, 102, 103, 104, 107, 108, 110, 111, 112, 113, 114, 115, 116, 117, 121, 123, 124, 125, 126, 127, 128, 129, 132, 134, 135, 136, 138, 139, 140, 141, 144, 145, 146, 147, 148, 149, 150, 153, 154, 156, 157, 158, 161, 162; Chaeyoung and 225, 226; Dahyun and 214, 216, 218, 219;

Jeongyeon and 173, 174, 176, 177, 178, 179; Jihyo and 200, 202, 203; Mina and 205, 207, 208, 209, 210, 211; Momo and 183, 184, 185, 186, 187; Nayeon and 168, 169, 170, 171–2; origins of 45–50; Sana and 189, 190, 192, 193, 194, 195; Tzuyu and 233–4, 235

One Day 15

'One in a Million' 77–8, 81, 88, 178, 209

'One More Time' 101, 102–3

'1 to 10' 81

'Only You' 97, 134, 167, 222–3

Oppa Thinking 108

'Oxygen' 160, 224

Page Two (EP) 67–8

'Page Two' (single) 61

Pink Lemonade' 119–20

'Pit-a-pat' 81

'Polish' 154

'Ponytail' 81

Popteen 99

PPAP (Pen Pineapple Apple Pen) 76

'Precious Love' 67, 224, 234

Produce 48 22

Produce 101 24

Psy 50; *Gangnam Style* 83, 143

Rado (Song Joo-young) 32

Rain 12, 31, 182

'Rainbow' 148, 170

Real Men 56, 217

Red Velvet 4, 7, 29, 50, 82, 169, 174, 218

Republic Records 159
Riho 14
'Rollin' 105, 234
Rosé 84
Running Man 4, 168, 176, 209, 217

Same Bed, Different Dreams 53
Sana 48, 49, 50, 56, 58, 59, 77, 79, 83, 86, 87, 89, 100, 108, 110, 114, 116, 122, 138, 146, 151, 155, 158, 176, 177, 179, 185, 189–95, 199, 200, 207, 215, 216, 218, 219; Akihito abdication and 139–40, 194; 'BDZ' and 125; 'Candy Pop' and 111; 'Cheer Up' and 60, 61, 62–3, 93, 189, 191–2; 'Feel Special' and 147, 195; 'Ice Cream' and 93; 'Likey' and 103, 195; 'One More Time' and 101; 'Pit-a-pat' and 81; 'Signal' and 96, 97, 98; 'Sleep Tight, Good Night' and 105; 'Sweet Talker' and 115; 'TT' and 78; 'Tuk Tok' and 67; 'Turn it Up' and 137; '21:29' and 149; Twice debut and 25, 26, 27, 30, 33, 36, 38, 40, 42, 43; Twice origins and background of 14, 15, 17, 18, 20, 21, 183, 190–1; 'Yes or Yes' and 127
San E 166
'Say It Again' 18, 125
'Say Yes' 115
'Say You Love Me' 128
SBS (Seoul Broadcasting System): Drama Awards 178; Entertainment Awards 178; *Gayo Daejun* 50, 83–4, 235
Sensei Kunshu (movie) 120

Seo Taiji 6
Seoul Music Awards 5, 132
S.E.S. 6, 160
Seungyeon 56, 157–8, 174, 175, 177, 178
Seventeen 46, 50, 84
SHINee 50, 55, 138
'Shot Thru The Heart' 122, 226
Show! Music Core 29, 38, 66
'Shy, Shy, Shy' meme 62–4, 66, 93, 191–2
Seize the Light 157, 161, 174, 175, 179
Signal (EP) 95–8, 201
'Signal' (single) 95–7, 99, 108, 116, 234
Sika 14
Simply K-pop 66
Sistar 32, 97
6Mix 13–15, 23, 167, 175, 190, 198, 199, 200
Sixteen 14–24, 25, 26, 27, 30, 33–4, 40, 57, 66, 67, 68, 76, 88, 131, 132, 146, 161, 167, 168, 170, 171, 175, 179, 182, 183, 186, 188, 190, 191, 193, 198, 201, 207, 210, 213, 215–16, 218, 219, 223, 230, 231
Skoolooks 40, 51, 54
'Sleep Tight, Good Night' 105
SM Entertainment 2, 12, 29, 82, 149–50, 174, 177, 178, 214
Snoopy: The Peanuts Movie 51
Sohee 12, 64
'Someone Like Me' 97, 116
Somi 16, 18, 20, 21, 24, 67, 207, 223
Son Dam-bi 57
'Stay By My Side' 126

'Strawberry' 137, 224
Stray Kids 7, 122, 224
'Stronger' 154
'Stuck' 115, 116, 122, 139
'Stuck in My Head' 137, 139
Summer Nights 122, 123
Sungkyu 41–2, 43
Sunmi 13, 84, 112, 202
'Sunset' 128, 201
Super Junior 6, 70–1, 156, 186
Superstar K 15, 183
'Sweet Summer Day' 160, 178, 224
'Sweet Talker' 115, 116, 178, 224
'Swing Baby' 182
Swing Entertainment 24

Taeyeon 37
Taiwan 11, 16, 18, 26, 44, 52, 54, 55, 85, 86, 229, 230, 231, 232, 235
TAK 89
T-ara 32
Ta-Mi 98
Teen Top 32
10cm 84
'The Best Thing I Ever Did' 132, 156
'The Reason Why' 154
The Show 38
The Story Begins 30, 33, 37
The Year of Yes 132
'Three Times a Day' 97, 209
'T' logo 138
Tokyo Dome 133
Tokyo Girls Collection 125
Top 3 Chef King 53
Touchdown in Japan 100

'Touchdown' 67, 87, 139, 183, 219, 224
trainees 2, 12, 13, 14, 15–16, 17, 18, 20, 21, 25, 39, 42, 58, 67, 72, 86, 88, 95, 132, 137, 157, 165, 166, 167, 168, 169, 174, 175, 182, 183, 185, 190, 191, 198, 199, 200, 202, 206, 207, 208, 214, 218, 222, 223, 230–1
Tranter, Justin 159
'Trick It' 78, 148, 209, 219
Trouble Maker 32
'Truth' 20, 33–4, 37
'TT' 76, 77, 78–81, 83, 84, 85, 88, 89, 91–2, 98, 99, 100, 103, 109, 110–11, 112, 135, 143, 179, 202, 209, 215, 216
TTS 71
'Tuk Tok' 67, 224
'Turn it Up' 81, 137
'Turtle' 104–5
TVXQ 46
'21:29' 149
'24/7' 105, 170, 201
Twice: albums *see individual album name*; awards/award shows *see individual award show name*; choreography 26, 27, 32, 34, 36, 38, 39, 41, 42, 49, 51, 56, 57, 63, 65, 67, 68, 71, 72, 79–80, 81, 82, 87, 92–3, 96, 101, 104, 108, 109–10, 112, 113, 121, 122, 124, 127, 136, 141, 149–50, 157, 158, 159, 167, 170–1, 181, 184, 185, 187, 190, 208, 209, 214, 219; colour pop 31, 32, 33, 37, 61; commercials 40, 76, 112, 119, 166; Covid-19 pandemic and

157; debut 28–34; debut stages (performances) 37–9; EPs *see individual EP name*; fan meetings 40, 45, 46, 69, 74, 102, 111, 150, 176, 233; J-line/J-Trinity 2, 59, 60, 86, 100, 122, 185, 193; magazine shoot, first 39–40; members 163–235 *see also individual member name*; music shows and *see individual music show name*; Once (Twice fandom) *see* Once; origins of 11–24; product endorsements 51, 52, 232; sales 68, 80–1, 92, 112, 122, 138, 140, 160; songs *see individual song name*; TikTok channel 158; tours *see individual tour name*; Twitter account 157; variety shows and *see individual variety show name*; videos 27, 29, 30–1, 32, 35–7, 44, 45, 48–9, 50, 51, 52, 53, 56, 58, 61–3, 65, 70, 71, 78, 80, 81, 83, 90–2, 96, 99, 101, 102, 103–4, 107, 109, 110, 111, 112, 113–14, 115, 116, 119, 120, 121, 124–5, 126, 127, 128, 131, 132, 133, 136, 137, 140, 141, 146, 147, 150, 153, 155, 157, 158, 159–60, 166, 167, 168, 170, 171, 175, 176, 178, 179, 184, 191, 219

#Twice 99–100

'Twice Avengers' 70

TWICEcoaster: Lane 1 76, 80–2, 83

TWICEcoaster: Lane 2 89–90, 93

Twicecoaster showcase 78

TwiceFriend 57

'Twiceland' 86–7

Twiceland – The Opening 87–9, 93–4

Twiceland – The Opening Encore 97–8

Twiceland Zone 2: Fantasy Park 115–17, 120

Twicelights tour 135, 138–9, 140–1, 143–5, 153–4, 156–7, 194, 202, 211, 226, 235

Twice's Elegant Private Life 57–9

TWICE Showcase Live Tour 2018 'Candy Pop' 112

Twicetagram 102–5, 110, 143, 178, 201

Twicetober 77

Twice TV 27–8, 40, 41, 74, 77, 93, 107

#Twice 2 134

Twice University Fashion Club 157

2AM 15, 198

2NE1 4, 6, 29, 97, 143, 222

2PM 12, 13, 15, 20, 31, 48, 50, 60, 73, 86, 95, 116, 182, 184, 190, 198, 202, 222

Tzuyu 48, 49, 50, 52, 53, 56, 57, 58, 59, 60, 62, 66, 70, 72, 76, 77, 78, 83, 86, 87, 98, 99–100, 107–8, 114, 116, 121, 122, 123, 132, 135, 139, 145, 150, 155, 157, 158, 177, 185, 200, 215, 218, 219, 222, 225, 229–35; 'Brand New Girl' and 112, 234; 'Candy Pop' and 111; 'Fancy' and 136; 'Feel Special' and 146, 147; 'Heart Shaker' and 109; 'Knock Knock' and 91, 92; 'Like Ooh Ahh' and 73; 'Likey' and 103, 104; *maknae* 25, 42, 57,

122, 123, 200, 229, 231–2, 233;
'Signal' and 96, 234; 'Tuk Tok'
and 67; 'Turtle' and 105;
TWICEcoaster: Lane 1 and 82;
Twice debut 25, 26, 27, 30, 36,
38, 40, 41, 42, 43, 167–8, 232,
234–5; Twice origins and
background of 16, 18, 19, 20, 21,
131, 230–2; waves flag of
independent Taiwan 52, 54, 55,
232, 235; 'Yes or Yes' and 126–7

variety shows 4–5 *see also
individual variety show name*
visuals (those whose looks alone
get them noticed) 2, 39, 171
Vitamin 74
Vivi 99
VIXX 50
V Live 5, 27–8, 31, 32, 46, 69, 73,
74, 77, 86, 89, 101, 107, 125, 126,
131, 156, 157, 161, 170, 185, 186,
187, 192, 201, 210, 216, 218, 225,
227, 235

'Wake Me Up' 119–20, 134
Wanna B 29

Wanna One 145, 202
We Are Siblings 56, 178
Weekly Idol 4, 41–4, 79, 108,
186–7, 217
What is Love? (EP) 113–15, 122
'What is Love?' (single) 113–15,
119, 129, 132, 171, 179, 184, 194,
208, 226
'What You Waiting For' 154
Who stole Once's heart? 102
'Wishing' 125
Wonder Girls 6, 12, 13, 19, 31, 49,
64, 66, 73, 84, 85, 95, 97, 143,
198, 202, 224

Yes or Yes (EP) 126–8, 132
'Yes or Yes' (single) 126–8, 179,
208, 216
YG Entertainment 2, 24, 29, 73,
82, 214
Y!Mobile 112
'Young and Wild' 128
YouTube 29, 35, 41, 43, 44, 52,
71, 76, 80, 83, 99, 104, 107, 109,
131, 133, 155, 157, 186, 216,
219
Yubin 73